Odin's Chosen

A Handbook of Ásatrú

Odin's Chosen

A Handbook of Ásatrú

Faolchú Ifreann and
Tyrsoak Josephsson

Hubbardston, Massachusetts

Asphodel Press
12 Simond Hill Road
Hubbardston, MA 01452

Odin's Chosen: A Handbook of Ásatrú
© 2015 Faolchú Ifreann and Tyrsoak Josephsson
ISBN 978-1-938197-14-7

Cover design by Tony Sahara.

Printed in cooperation with
Lulu Enterprises, Inc.
3101 Hillsborough St.
Raleigh, NC 27607-5436

Dedicated to all the proud men and women who, through word and deed, reawakened the religion of Ásatrú throughout Midgard, and to Jay Nink III, Aidan Bankovic, and Andrew Bankovic, the future of our Folk.

Contents

Acknowledgements..i
Foreword I iii
Mission Statement v
Foreword II.. vi

Ásatrú

Odin's Chosen 1
Faolchú's Morning Salutation 5
Sigdrifa's Prayer... 6
A History of Ásatrú.. 8
The Norse Creation Myth... 11
Ragnarök.. 13
Gods, Goddesses, and Wights 16
Yggdrasill and the Nine Worlds 32
The Soul... 35
The Afterlife.. 36
The Nine Noble Virtues 37
The Rede of Honor for Odinism 39
The Six-Fold Goal... 41
Nine-Step Guide to Establishing an Ásatrú Group in Prison 43

Runic Work

The Runes 53
The Elder Futhark 56
Rune Creation Ritual 69
Rune Creation Ritual If Incarcerated 71
Rune Casting Ritual.. 73

Rituals

Ritual: Blót, Feast, and Sumbel.................................... 79
Nine-Step Blót Format 83
Ritual Tools... 85
Kindred-Recognized Holy Days 87
Seasonal Rituals 98
Snowmoon/January: Charming of the Plow................ 98

Horning/February: Sigrblót 102
Lenting/March 20: Spring Equinox and Feast of Ostara 105
Lenting/March 17: Birth of Our Kindred 109
Fast To Celebrate The Birth Of Our Kindred 116
April/Ostara: Blót to Thor 118
Merrymoon/May 1: May Day 123
Midyear/June 21: Midsummer (Summer Solstice) 126
Haymoon/July: Thing Blót 130
Harvest/August: Freyfaxi 134
Shedding/September 20 or 21: Winterfinding, the Autumnal
    Equinox 138
Hunting/October: Disablót 143
Fogmoon/November 11: Odin Blót and Feast of Einherjar 145
Yule/December 20 or 21: Winter Solstice 149
Yule/December 31: Twelfth Night 154

Other Rites
Rites of Passage Used by the Guardians of Othala 163
Rite of Self-Profession 163
Rite of Fostering 164
Rite of Profession to the Kindred 165
Hammer Ritual 167
Solitary Blóts 173
Burial Customs 174

Sacred Lands
Our Sacred Land 179
Sacred Places in Ásatrú 181
The Meaning of a Sacred Place 185
Construction of a Ritual Area 193
Land Claiming Ritual 196

Appendixes
Appendix I: Proposal For Starting a Kindred 201
Appendix II: Membership in Guardians of Othala Kindred 204
Appendix III: Kindred Structure 207
Appendix IV: Our Kindred Oath 210

Appendix V: Old Norse Pronunciation 211
Appendix VI: Dietary Standards... 212
Appendix VII: Divine Association Runes and Colors................ 213
Appendix VIII: The Futhorc Runes... 214
Appendix IX: The Younger Futhark... 216
Appendix X: The Anglo-Saxon Rune Poem 217
Appendix XI: Sigdrifa's Prayer Choral Music 225
Appendix XII: Guardians of Othala Contact Information.......... 229

Livestock die,
Friends and family die,
One day we too will die,
But our fame and honor will live forever.

-The Hávamál

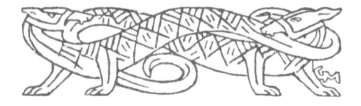

Acknowledgements

The Guardians of Othala would like to give a special thanks to all the people who have helped us in our walk along this path. For without you, we would not have the knowledge or energy to even begin a book like this. Some of you are family, friends, and fellow ASA Folk. Some have written books that strengthened our knowledge and inspired us to look deeper into the mysteries of our lives. Others have shown us through word or deed how to uphold the Odinist principles we hold so dear. You have all made a difference in our lives and will forever remain in our hearts and thoughts. May we all continue to strive to strengthen our folk.

Our Kindred would like to raise a horn in honor of:

Valgard Murray and his family, Stephen McNallen and his family, Ron McVan and his family, The Brüder Schweigen, SveinbJorn Beinteinsson, Else Christensen, Thorsteinn Thorarinsson, Edred Thorsson, Guido Von List, Lee M. Hollander, Dr. Mark L. Mirabello, Freya Aswyn, Diane Paxson, Winfred Hodge, Carl Jung, Raven Kaldera and Asphodel Press, and the Outreach Ministry of the Ásatrú Alliance.

Faolchú Ifreann, Cheiftain of Guardians of Othala Kindred, would like to thank his loving wife Sarah, for without her this book would not be published. His mother Mary and sister Amy for their constant loving support. His grandmother Mary Ellen and father Walter who left this world too early. They are truly missed. For the seeds of esoteric wisdom that were planted in his youth, he would like to honor: The Order of the Ancients, Aleister Crowley, MacGregor Mathers, Kenneth Grant, Dr. John Dee and Edward Kelly, Don Webb, Michael Bertieaux, and Michael Ford, Paul and Jack from Aurum Solis bookstore, Viktor Rydberg, Edred Thorsson, and Guido Von List. Faolchú would like to send a special thank you to Richard Scutari, for the sacrifices he has made for the Folk. Last but not least he would like to thank Daniel Moreschi for the artwork in this book.

Tyrsoak Josephsson, Goði of Guardians of Othala, would like to thank his grandmother Loretta Bailey for her never failing love and wisdom. His four children William, Stephanie, Mark, and Steve. His brothers of the old Raven Wolf Kindred in F.C.I. Pekin 1997-2009. Joe Miller who fostered him, and Rob Wirth who has left us for the halls of his ancestors. Dot and Dewey Prins who loved me as their own son. To Olga Cunningham who will always hold a special place in my heart and Angela Brezewski Dauska who gave me many happy memories. To the many others who have touched my life in some way, for without you I would not be the man I am today. May my words and deeds make you proud.

foreword I

Tyrsoak Josephsson and Faolchú Ifreann

The book you now hold in your hands was written in hopes of helping men and women rediscover the path their ancestors laid down for them thousands of years ago. This book contains knowledge that will give you not just the basic lore, but some deeper meaning and insights to get you started. Take what you read here and add your own insight, gather knowledge from other books and keep gaining and growing in the way of life called Ásatrú. We don't have any one book we consider our holy text or a book we're told contains all the answers. Instead, we have men and women who have taken wisdom our ancestors left for us and applied it to their own lives, and then put down in words their experiences for us to learn from. Together we help to reawaken that spark of divinity which is within us all.

Tyrsoak: Ten years ago, as Goði of the Raven Wolf Kindred, I wrote *Handbook of Ásatrú* and *Our Sacred Land* in hopes of helping others beginning their walk upon this path learn some of the basic lore of Ásatrú. I was truly blessed by the responses I received, so I have decided to update a lot of the text and include it as part of *Odin's Chosen*, as we learn and grow our way of looking at things will change and that's the whole idea behind this way of life. It's doing whatever it takes to gain new wisdom and use it to change your life for the better. In doing so, you will also be changing things for those around you. Your family and folk and the cycle goes on and on; each one of us doing our part to make this world a better place for those who will come after us. We honor our ancestors by our words and deeds. Hail to those who strive to honor the Old Ones.

Faolchú: There have been hundreds of excellent books written about Odinism, Ásatrú, and Northern Tradition Paganism. I have learned valuable information from each one I've read. We are very lucky to have so many outstanding authors writing about our religion and way of life today. When Tyrsoak and I discussed writing *Odin's Chosen*, we wanted to write a practical book that would give the reader all the tools necessary to connect with the Gods of our ancestors and start them on their path of Ásatrú.

We took the *Handbook of Ásatrú* and used it as a basic framework to expand upon. We didn't want to just update some of the content, we wanted to apply new knowledge and a fresh perspective to create something better. I feel we have.

We have tried to make *Odin's Chosen* a one-stop source for knowledge on:

- The Gods, Goddesses and wights.
- The Nine Worlds.
- The Runes.
- The Soul Complex.
- The rituals.
- Our calendar and our values.

Inside you will find a step-by-step guide to making your own runes, performing Blóts and awakening your Thor's Hammer. We also have included a guide to establish a kindred inside prison, and sections of *Our Sacred Land*.

We hope that this information will help the Ásatrúar both inside and outside of prison. If the information in here helps just one person connect with the Old Ones, then this endeavor has truly been a fruitful one.

If you like what have read and want to become a member of our kindred, you can contact us at:

Guardians of Othala
P.O. Box 216
Downers Grove, IL 60515

Mission Statement

Faolchú Ifreann, Tyrsoak Josephsson, and Jay Nink Jr. formed The Guardians of Othala Kindred to serve as a beacon of hope and a vehicle of change for like-minded Odinists/Ásatrúar and their families. The Guardians of Othala are an Ásatrú Alliance kindred based in Illinois and we now have members in several states. Since many of our members are scattered throughout the U.S., we do not hold scheduled meetings. Instead, we simply insist that members Blót on our Holy Days and stay in contact with us. Our kindred is a spiritual entity that binds its members together so that no distance can break that bond. Through this bond, right action, noble conduct, and the Web of Wyrd, we will one day meet on the Plain of Vigriðr to join forces with Odin and the Einherjar to do battle against the Baningar.

foreword II

Valgard Murray

Not very long ago, Ásatrú was reintroduced to the Northern European peoples. After a dormancy of centuries imposed on us by those who served the jealous gods, the Ásatrú once again are rediscovering their native spirituality and indigenous folkways and are openly and proudly worshipping their ancestral Gods and Goddesses.

In my more than thirty-five years of service to my people, I have seen the Ásatrú community grow from a mere handful of stalwart pioneers to a thriving nation of hundreds of kindreds and thousands of practitioners of the old ways, not only here in Vinland, but throughout Midgard as well. Would there be any doubt that this spiritual revival would encompass every strata of our people? This would include prisoners in the federal and state-managed prisons to who I have ministered to for over twenty-five years.

Odin's Chosen is a result of that devotion to duty shown by so many kindreds in the penal institutions here in Vinland. Faolchú and Tyrsoak have devoted their lives to service to the High Ones and the Tru Folk, and this work is a testament to that devotion. After hundreds of hours of serious study, research, practice, and living the old ways of our ancestors, the members of Guardians of Othala of the Ásatrú Alliance have produced this endeavor to aid prisoners and administrators alike to better understand the mechanics of Ásatrú and the importance of the Ásatrú Kindred. However, I believe that all kindreds and members of Odin's Nation in the free world will also benefit from the contents of this book and find it to be a valued resource of both information and inspiration. This manuscript is published in the spirit of kinship and solidarity to all who follow the ancient ways of their noble ancestors.

Valgard Murray
Director of World Tree Publications
Allshergothi, Ásatrú Alliance
Haymoon 27, 2264 Runic Era

Ásatrú

Odin's Chosen

Odin's chosen are the Einherjar, those great warriors slain in battle and carried by the Valkyries to the halls of Valhalla. There, we are told, they fight all day and feast all night, telling the tales of their great battles and deeds of great renown that made them worthy of a place in Valhalla, the hall of the chosen slain. The history of the Vikings have many tales of warriors talking of Valhalla and their willingness to fight in battle after battle in hopes of earning a place there and to be reunited with family and friends they feel already have gained acceptance in the ranks of the Einherjar.

For thousands of years children have heard stories of great warriors and battles they have fought, lands they have conquered, and riches they gained. It is these stories that inspire those young children to dream of becoming great warriors themselves, and go on to do even greater deeds than those they read about. It's this inspiration that leads many to do things never considered possible, to become the heroes of today and the stories that will be written and read about tomorrow.

What is it that makes a person a hero? Is it fighting in a great battle, or risking life or limb to save someone? Doing something so brave that no one would dare try it? What do you think of when you picture a hero or a warrior worthy of a place in the halls of Valhalla? We could come up with a lot of different answers, and I believe that is the whole point. Warriors and heroes are viewed differently throughout history. Today, many argue that it is only the brave men and women in the armed services who can die in battle and thus get a chance to go to the halls of Valhalla, and in a sense that's true, to a point. But that is only one kind of battle, and there are many battles being fought today, as well as many types of warriors. Let us look at a few here, understanding that there are many others.

Men and Women of the Armed Forces

There can be no doubt that these brave men and women who risk life and limb to protect our great country and the freedoms that we have are worthy warriors, whatever role they play in the battle. They are out there on the front lines defending their families and ours so we can continue to enjoy the freedoms and everything else our great country offers. Raise a horn to these warriors whenever the opportunity arises.

Doctors, Nurses, and other Medical Professionals

We honor those in the medical profession who give their all to finding new cures and combating disease on a daily basis. Some dedicate their entire lives to seeking a cure or new procedure to save lives. Other work in hospitals, clinics, or homecare doing their best to provide the care people need to overcome sickness, disease, and death. Hail to those who give their all to help those in need.

Firemen and Law Enforcement

We honor those brave men and women who risk their lives to save or protect us and our families in times of danger. Those in this profession take an oath to serve and protect, and as long as they live up to that oath and do not become corrupt due to outside influences, we must be thankful for their protection. Those who abuse their authority or violate their oath and disgrace their profession should be deemed oathbreakers.

Politicians

We honor those men and women who stay true to their word once elected, and fight to make sure the Constitutional rights our ancestors fought and died for are not taken from us. Many battles are fought in this arena, and we hail those that take on the opposing factions and outside influences that seek to steal away the rights and liberties we hold to be a sacred trust passed on to us from our ancestors. Vote for those who stay true to their word and support them in any way you can.

Attorneys

We hail those men and women who have taken an oath to uphold the law honorably, and will fight for what is right and just. With the energy of the God Tyr, justice will win out! Many in this field can become corrupted by outside influences and the greed to acquire wealth, but there are others who stay true and will do their best to seek fairness and justice on both sides. These are the warriors and lawspeakers we honor today.

Inventers/Scientists/Researchers

We hail those men and women who discover new ways to improve life for us in today's world. They give us not just all those conveniences that make us lazy, but rather those things that allow people to live longer, to do things they would not otherwise be able to do (such as walk, see, hear, move, drive, and take care of themselves rather than be dependent on anyone). Their work may cover anything from aerospace, computers, tools, transportation, and so on. Honor those who have sometimes spent years on an idea to make things better for their fellow man.

Historians/Artists/Writers

We hail the men and women who do their part to keep the old ways alive, through looking back at what our ancestors left and recording it so others can look at it and learn from it. I believe these people probably inspire us more than any others, as it is through their media that we see, hear, or read something that opens our eyes and reawakens that spark of divinity within. It is through them that we discover all the others who have done something worthy to be remembered. Hail to all those who bring the old ways to life.

Mothers/Fathers/Other Family Members

These men and women are the backbone of our folk, whether as parents, uncles, aunts, grandparents, etc. Their work should be stepping up to help family in need, and doing it unselfishly. Many family members have gone to bed hungry so that others could eat, or worked two jobs so others could go to school or have a place to live and clothes on their backs. It is these individuals we never forget. We can all relate to the difficulties facing families today in our society. It touches us all, and some battles are fought on a day to day basis. Hail these warriors and send them some energy to help as they strive to overcome what brings their family down.

Special Note: Kindreds, tribes, and clans are all considered extended family, as they fill many of the same roles as above, so remember to raise a horn to them as well.

You, the reader of this book

Yes, you have it in yourself to be a hero, to be a warrior of the folk, and to do your part to keep the old ways alive. Ásatrú—"True to the Aesir"—starts here; let it be seen in your life as an example for others to see. Share the knowledge you learn with family and friends. Whatever you do, do it to the best of your ability. In all areas of your life, do what it takes to overcome any negativity in your life, and strive forward to better yourself in any way that you can.

For many people, mere everyday life can be a battle, so remember to help those struggling around you. We are in this together and there is strength in numbers. That's why kindreds are formed—so we can be around like-minded individuals who are striving and facing the same kind of difficulties. We bond together to overcome that which seeks to hold us back. Through the wisdom of Odin, the strength of Thor, the boldness of Baldr, and the victory of Tyr we will overcome. We will remain the Guardians of Othala—Odin's Chosen.

Faolchú's Morning Salutation

This is the prayer that Faolchú uses first thing in the morning to connect with the Gods.

Stand facing north and close your eyes. Envision a bright white orb the size of your fist hovering above your head. This orb symbolizes the Holy Light of Asgard. With your sword hand, reach up and wrap your hand around it. Feel the warmth. Slowly begin to pull this energy down to you. Rotate your fist so that your thumb's first knuckle is pointed towards you. (It is easier to draw runes with your thumb like this.) Pull the energy down to your forehead, mark the Ansuz rune, and then say:

"Odin, Wotan, Warrior of warriors, Lord of hosts, terror of Asgard's foes be thou honored. All-Father, Harr, Ordeal Master, and winner of the runes, guide me this day. God of magic, impart upon me your wisdom. Battle master, wielder of Gungnir, lead me to victory."

Pull the energy down to your mouth and mark the Fehu rune, then say:

"Freya, Vanadís, Gefn, luck bringer, be thou hailed! Goddess of Seiðr, teach me the secret words of your magic. Goddess of war, Queen of Valkyries, lend me your shield. Gird and guide me to be victorious today."

Pull the energy down to your heart and mark the Uruz rune. Then say:

"Baldr, I call upon you who waits imprisoned in Hel's dark halls. Empower me with your courage and perserverance. Great teacher, lend me your endurance and fortitude so that my spirit cannot be broken."

Pull the energy over to your left shoulder and mark the Thurisaz rune, then say:

"Thor, Thunar, Red-Beard, be thou hailed! Wielder of Mjölnir, I fear nothing with you on my side. Protector of Midgard, lend me your strength to break down any barrier in my path."

Pull the energy to your right shoulder and mark the Teiwaz rune, then say:

"Tyr, God of justice, sacrifice and right action, I honor you. Lord of Swords, One-Handed God, give me the courage to do what must be done. God of Honor, lead me along the path of right action and help me do what is right in the face of all fear."

Then say Sigdrifa's prayer and begin the day with the blessings of the Gods.

Sigdrifa's Prayer

Sigdrifa, also known as Brynhild, is one of the most famous Valkyries in Norse Literature. She witnessed a man named Agnar losing a battle against Hjalmgunnar, a much stronger warrior. Sigrdrifa came to his defense and slew Hjalmgunnar, who unbeknownst to her was promised victory by Odin. The All-Father, instead of ending her life, put her to sleep with a sleep thorn and forever retired her from battle.

Sigurð, the hero of the Volsung saga, while riding over Hindar-fells, came upon a wall of shields shining so brightly it blinded him momentarily. He cautiously approached and found an unconscious Valkyrie in full battle gear. He took off her helmet and removed her armor. Sigdrifa awoke and recited the following stanzas that comprise Sigdrifa's prayer, which is the oldest prayer our people have. (Note: some translations may differ.)

Hail day
Hail Day's sons
Hail Night and her daughter
Look upon me with loving eyes
That waiting I gain victory.

Hail all the Gods and Goddesses
Hail the generous Earth
Give me goodly speech
And healing hands life long.

When reciting this prayer, our kindred customizes it by adding the following lines:

"Sigrdrífa, victory bringer, inciter to victory, I hail you. Grant me victory in all my actions today."

(Choral music for an arrangement of Sigdrifa's Prayer was donated to this book by Raven Kaldera and Galina Krasskova. It can be found in the appendix section.)

A History of Ásatrú

Valgard Murray, Director of World Tree Publications,
Allshejargoði, Ásatrú Alliance of Independent Kindreds

As I attempt to look back on the history of Ásatrú and place an exact date on its beginnings, I find myself in awe at how long our ancestors have been living the way of life we now call Ásatrú. For those of us who are descendants of those proud people, we know that they hailed from many lands, including the British Isles, the Scandinavian countries, the Netherlands, the Germanic countries: France, Austria, Switzerland, the Baltic States, Northern Russia, Poland, and numerous other countries. We can rest assured that our way of life and religion is far older than most people think.

Some speculate that Ásatrú as an organized religion is at least eight thousand years old. This would make it older than most organized religions today. It is also believed by many that Northern Europeans have been honoring the Gods and Goddesses in one way or another, since our people came into existence. I believe we can safely say that our religion is by far one of the oldest in existence today. and as such deserves the respect given to all the other, far younger, yet more widely recognized religions.

As our ancestors spread throughout all of Midgard, they carried with them that spark of divinity within. In some parts of the world our way of life evolved and the Gods and Goddesses were given different names, and some took on various aspects from other parts of the world where the culture and customs were different. Yet within our very souls they remained, evolving just as we were.

The sagas, myths and Eddas tell us of the proud people that lived our way of life long ago. They show us the aspects of the Gods and Goddesses that give us meaning for our lives today. Our ancestors— like us today—could envision the various struggles our Gods and Goddesses went through. We look at the symbolism and allegories to discover the meaning in our lives today. just as our ancestors did many years ago.

Times are changing, and many people are beginning to discover that their connection to the better-known religions is shallow, and that something is still missing in their lives. I believe it is that connection and bond to the holy ones and Old Ways that our ancestors always had until a new and foreign religion came along and attempted to sever that bond. In many cases they were successful. yet in many lands there were some that remained true to the Old Ways and kept the Gods and Goddesses alive. Despite this persecution, however, elements of Ásatrú continued down to our own times, often in the guise of folklore.

Norse myths are stories about the Gods and Goddesses of Ásatrú. Worshippers believe these are ways of stating religious truths. Myths contain truths about the nature of divinity, the nature of huMánity, and the relationship between the two.

We believe in an underlying, all-pervading divine energy or essence which is generally hidden because it surpasses direct human understanding. We also believe that our spiritual reality is interdependent with us—that we affect it and it affects us. This underlying divinity expresses itself to us in the forms of the Gods and Goddesses. Stories about the Norse Gods are to us like a sort of code—the "mysterious language". We do not contend that the myths are literally true as history, but to us the Gods and Goddesses are real. However, just as most Christians do not think that their God is really an old bearded figure sitting on a golden chair in heaven, we do not believe Thórr, for example, is actually a muscular, man-shaped entity carrying a big hammer. There is a real Thor, but we approach an understanding of him through a particular mental picture.

Still, followers of Ásatrú pray to their Gods and Goddesses. We never surrender our will to theirs or humble ourselves before them, because we see ourselves as their kin, not as their property, or so our tenets proclaim. Nor do we beg and plead. We do, however, commune with them through formal rites and through informal meditations.

Actually, we believe that living a full and virtuous life is a form of prayer. Our religion should affect all parts of our lives, not just some fragments that we choose to call "religious". We do not worship stones and trees and statues, but these are important symbols. We know that trees, wooden statues, the sun and other natural or man-made objects are not gods. So we don't worship them. We do sometimes use these items as reminders of a God or Goddess, and we believe they can become "charged" with a certain aspect of the divine energy.

Ásatrú holds in high regard the qualities of strength, courage, joy, honor, freedom, loyalty to kin, realism, vigor and the honoring of our ancestors. We strive to express these qualities in our lives, and minimize what we see as vices—weakness, cowardice, and adherence to dogma rather than to realities. More recently, a few people stand out that we feel have had that eternal flame rekindled within, and then watched as it was spread to others who began to search out the religion and way of life of their ancestors that we now call Ásatrú.

They are our modern day heroes, who have sacrificed much and often watch as others take credit for their hard work: Else Christensen, the mother of modern day Ásatrú; Sveinbjorn Beinteinsson and Thorsteinn Thorarinsson, two men that helped our way of life emerge again in the lands of our ancestors: Stephen McNallen of the A.F.A. who helped reawaken so many in our own Vinland starting in the early seventies; Valgard Murray of the Ásatrú Alliance, who has fought many battles for our Folk over the years trying to get Ásatrú recognized throughout all of Vinland: Edred Thorsson, whose writings on the Runes have opened the eyes of many who now realize they already have the keys to the mysteries hidden within: Max Hyatt, whose writings and support gave many a strong foundation as they began their walk upon the path. There are many others I'm sure that we haven't heard of and we thank you all. for without you the history of Ásatrú would remain history instead of reemerging as the living and breathing entity of Asa-Folk everywhere. Hail the Gods and Goddesses!

The Norse Creation Myth

Note: There have been numerous translations of the "Codex Regius", which contains many of our stories such as the creation of the Nine Worlds and the origin of Mankind. Some of these translations can be confusing because of the poor condition of the original manuscript, and because some words or phrases in the Old Norse language do not have English equivalents. This has caused some controversy regarding which translation is the most accurate representation of the original manuscript. Every translation is fundamentally similar in structure and content, but each one has subtle differences. We encourage you to read and compare some of them and make your own interpretation. The following is Faolchú's interpretation of the creation story.

In the beginning, there was only the Mighty Gap, Ginnungagap; the primordial void. Within boiled a chaotic, magical energy where there was neither existence nor nonexistence. Inside this vortex, an Ash seed formed and began to germinate and grow into what would become the World Tree Yggdrasill. This same creative force spawned the first two realms. One, composed of fire, heat and brilliant light, called Múspellheim, drifted to the South. The other realm— Niflheim—was dark, cold and filled with ice and mist; it drifted to the North.

As eons passed, a spring called Hvergelmir bubbled to the surface of Niflheim and created a river of icy poison. This river, called Élivágar, flowed into the gap and froze. Vapor arose from Élivágar and created rime, which froze as well. Hot air and sparks drifted into the gap from Múspellheim and melted the rime into mist. Then the atmosphere inside the gap charged it with life, and it fell back down to create Ymir, also known as Aurgelmir. Ymir was a frost Jötun of incredible size, but he lacked any intelligence. He was born from the gap to be a conduit for creation, so Ymir slept and sweated. From his left armpit a boy grew and from his right a girl. Ymir's feet rubbed together and produced a six-headed giant. They coupled and created the race of the frost Jötnar.

Ginnungagap created a cow named Auðumbla from the same process so that Ymir would not starve. In his sleep, Ymir suckled from her udders, while Auðumbla licked the rime for her sustenance. As she licked she uncovered the hair of a man. The second day she licked enough rime to reveal his head. On the third day she licked the remaining ice away to reveal the first human, Búr, also known as Valtam.

Búr, created by the magic of Ginnungagap, awoke and fed off Auðumbla's milk, and mingled with the Jötnar. He met a beautiful giantess named Bestla, the daughter of Bolthorn. They married and had three sons: Odin, Vili and Vé. Their sons had the strength and magical potential of their mother, but the human features of their father.

As Odin and his brothers grew, so did the Jötun population of Ginnungagap. It grew so much that more land was needed, so the brothers devised a plan to slay the sleeping giant and use his body to create more land. They slew Ymir and began dividing his colossal body into sections, but his body produced so much blood that it flooded the gap. Odin and his brothers quickly began attaching sections of Ymir to Yggdrasilll to try to save the drowning Jötnar. They were too late, for all but two Jötnar drowned; Bergelmir and his wife survived by getting into a hollowed out tree and used it as a canoe. They washed up on a piece of Ymir's back that was attached to Yggdrasilll and began to repopulate it. They called it Jötunheim.

As they were creating the worlds, they noticed that maggots in Ymir's flesh begin to evolve into Dwarves. Odin and his brothers granted them intelligence and offered them their own world. In exchange, four Dwarves—Norðri, Suðri, Austri, and Vestri—would have to hold up Ymir's skull to make the sky that covers all the worlds. They agreed, and the dwarves were given Svartalfheim, which was made from Ymir's lower spine.

Next, Odin and his brothers flung Ymir's brains in the sky to create clouds. Then they collected sparks from Múspellheim and scattered them about to make stars. From Ymir's eyelashes, they made Midgard for the sons of Man; they created Asgard from Ymir's neck bones. Ymir's pelvis was used to create Vanaheim. Ljóssálfheim was also created, but there is no documentation on which parts were used.

When they were finally done creating the worlds, they walked on the beach of Midgard where they came across two logs, one of Ash and the other an Elm. (Some translations say that both were Ash.) Odin breathed life into them, creating a man from the Ash and a woman from the Elm. Vili gave them intelligence and Vé gave them their speech, hearing, and sight. The brothers named them Ask and Embla and sent them on their way to populate Midgard with the race of Man.

Their last effort of creation was the Sun and Moon. Two spheres were fashioned, one from elements of Múspellheim and the other from Niflheim. Once they were created, Odin and his brothers made chariots to pull them through the sky across the Nine Worlds , but they had no one to drive them. Eventually they came across a Jötun called Mundilfari, who had named his daughter Sunna (Sun) and his son Máni (Moon). Odin put them into the chariots, fettered magical horses to them, and tasked them to drive the chariots across the sky until Ragnarök.

Ragnarök

Ragnarök, which means "The Fate of the Gods", is comprised of a series of cataclysmic events that will lead to the destruction of the Gods and Mankind. The "Codex Regius" says that the first sign of the coming apocalypse will be three winters back to back without spring or summer. This time will be called the *Fimbulvetr* or "chief of winters", and will be filled with senseless bloodshed and lawlessness. Brother will kill brother, rivers will overflow, disease and famine will be rampant, and the laws of morality will be abandoned. The sun will rarely shine, and when it does it will produce blood-red sunsets.

Denizens of the other worlds will read the signs and prepare for the final battle. The dwarves in Svartalfheim will groan and secure themselves behind the stone doors of their grottoes. Horror will spread through Hel as the souls are packed into Naglfari, the ship of the dead. In Jötunheim, Hrym will prepare the giants for battle. Then Fenris' sons, Sköll and Hati, will swallow the sun and moon, plunging all the worlds into darkness and chaos. Yggdrasill will shake, causing earthquakes that will topple mountains, uproot trees and break all restraints, which will free Fenris and Loki from their prisons. Garm, Hel's blood-stained watchgard, will howl from Gnipahellir and run free. Men and women who know the secrets of the runes will use the Bifröst Bridge to travel to safety.

In Jötunheim, Eggþér "the sword bearer" will play his harp, and Fjalar the red rooster will crow, signaling the call to final battle. The Aesir's golden rooster Gullinkambi which sits atop Valhalla will crow, and then Heimdall will sound the Gjallarhorn. Jörmungand will thrash in the oceans, sending tidal waves throughout Midgard, and will spray its poisonous venom across the land, further decimating the population. Naglfar, the ship made entirely from the toenails and fingernails of the Dead, will launch from Hel with Loki steering it. Hrym will come from the East with his shield before him and legions of giants behind him. Surt will march from the South with his flaming sword, with an army of fire giants from Múspellheim in tow. Surt's army is so massive that their combined weight will collapse the section of the Bifröst Bridge that connects Múspellheim to the other worlds.

Odin will consult with Mimir's head one last time, then the gods and the Einherjar (Odin's chosen) will prepare for final battle. With Gungnir in hand, Odin will lead the gods into battle on Vígriðr, a field in Asgard one hundred leagues in length. A ferocious battle will ensue and Odin will be swallowed by Fenris. Odin's son Viðarr, will avenge his death by tearing Fenris' jaws open and stabbing him in the heart. Thor will kill Jörmungand, but succumb to its poison within nine steps. Garm and Tyr will slay each other, as will Loki and Heimdall. Frey will battle Surt, but without his sword he will be slain. Surt, the sole survivor, will cover everything with an all-consuming fire. After the fire has snuffed out Mankind, Midgard will fall into the seas.

One day Midgard will rise from the seas and be fertile again. Crops will grow on unsown fields and the grass will be vibrant and green. The remaining gods will meet in Asgard in a field called Itha, where they will talk about Ragnarök, Jörmungand and the runes. Baldr and Höðr will return from Hel and join Viðar, Váli, Moði, and Magni in creating a new Asgard. Two humans—a male and female, Líf and Lífþrasir—will return from hiding within Yggdrasill's leaves and begin to repopulate Midgard. Sunna's daughter will emerge and take her place above Yggdrasill, providing light for all. Our ancient texts do not tell of the fates of the other worlds, so we are left to speculate.

Gods, Goddesses, and Wights

Our ancestors believed in a number of Gods, Goddesses, and Wights. Some of us think of them as real in the most literal sense, while others view them as archetypes that represent the divine aspects of the Universe. However you choose to experience them is completely up to you.

The following section is by no means a complete listing, nor is it an exhaustive list of each God or Goddesses talents or attributes. It is to serve as a primer to put the reader in touch with the ones our kindred works with. We urge the beginning Ásatrúar to do additional research by reading the Sagas and Eddas to further familiarize yourself with them.

The primary Gods and Goddesses belong to specific tribes or families. The gods of Asgard are referred to as the "Aesir", while the gods of Vanaheim are called the "Vanir". The third tribe are the "giants" or "Jötnar" from Jötunheim. The gods of the Aesir had been warring with the Vanir for ages until they came to a stalemate and hostages were exchanged and a peace accord was reached. However, the "giants" or "Jötnar" are considered by some to be the enemy of both the Aesir and Vanir due to their destructive temperament. Others consider the main Gods of the Jötnar (Loki, Hel, etc.) to be worthy of worship, and refer to them as the Rökkr (shadow Gods).

Through the study of Ásatrú/Odinist literature and personal gnosis (meditation) we can learn to emulate qualities of our gods, such as courage, honor, strength, freedom, the importance of family and ancestral bonds—but most importantly the preservation of our kind and our way of life.

Gods and Goddesses

Aegir: Also named Gymir or Hlér, he a sea-giant; God of the ocean and king of all sea creatures. He has an ale-hall (Aegirheim) where he brews ale for the gods. Aegir is married to Rán, the sea goddess who gathers the drowned souls in her fishing net. Aegir and Ran have nine daughters who are the Mánifestation of waves: Kolga, Dúfa, Blóðughadda, Hefring, Hronn, Bylgja, Bára, Unn, and Himinglaeva.

Angrboða: A Jötun (giantess) known as the "Old One" and the Mother of the Iron Wood clan. The Iron Wood is a forest in Jötunheim that is home to monsters and shapeshifters. In Old Norse her name means "bringer of grief", which can be an attestation of not only her temperament, but of the destruction her children are fated to bring about at Ragnarök. As one of Loki's wives, she bore him three children: Fenris, Hel, and Jörmungand (the Midgard serpent). Some practitioners of Rökkatru (worship of the Jötnar) look to her as a nurturing mother goddess much like the Aesir Frigg.

Baldr: The "Blameless One" is the son of Odin and Frigg. In Old Norse his name means "bold one" or "brave one"; it can also translate to "lord of men", "lord of warriors" and even "the white" or "the good". Baldr is married to Nanna; their son is Forseti the god of Justice. In some literature Baldr is the most beautiful of all Aesir. He lived in a palace called Breiðablik, which is so beautiful it is compared to the heavens.

One night he and his mother Frigg shared the same dream about his death. Frigg immediately went out to protect her son from harm and made every living thing vow to never hurt him. All things made this vow, except for mistletoe. Being so small and unassuming, Frigg thought nothing of it. However, hearing that mistletoe could harm Baldr, Loki made a spear with a sprig of mistletoe in its tip. He took this spear to the site where Baldr was letting the gods hit him with all manner of weapons as a game, because he was now impervious to almost everything. Loki handed the spear to Baldr's blind brother Höðr, who innocently hurled it at his brother and killed him.

Baldr's body was placed in his ship Hringhorni, the greatest ship ever built. As he was carried to his funeral ship, Odin whispered the eighteenth rune charm into his ear, then Baldr was ceremonially burnt. Thor kicked the dwarf Litr into the funeral pyre and Nanna threw herself into the flames to be with Baldr.

Later, Frigg sent Hermóðr to Hel to beg for her son's release from the underworld. Hel promised to release him if all things dead and alive would weep for him. All the creatures did, except for a giantess named Thökk, which was really Loki in disguise. So Baldr waits in the underworld until Ragnarök is over where he, Höðr and Thor's sons Magni and Móði will create the new world.

Bragi: Known as the greatest Skald and the god of poetry and eloquence, he gained his Skaldic talent after his wife, Iðunn, carved the runes into his tongue. Bragi is the son of Odin and the giantess Gunnlöð.

Dagr: Son of Nát. His name means day in Old Norse. He illuminates the sky in his chariot drawn by his steed, Skinfaxi.

Fárbauti: The Jötun god of thunder and lightning, he is a master of warcraft and plaguecraft. He is often called upon in rites of hexcraft by invoking the Sowelo rune. In Old Norse his name means "cruel striker". Fárbauti is the husband of Laufey and the father of Loki. Some Rokkatruar consider him to be the equivalent of the Aesir Thor.

Fenris: The Fenris wolf is one of Loki and Angrboða's three children. Fenris has other names in Norse mythology, such as:

Fenrir: Old Norse for "Fen Dweller"
Fenrisúlfr: Old Norse for "Fenris Wolf"
Hróðvitnir: Old Norse for "Famed Wolf"
Vánagandr: Old Norse for "Monster of the Ván", which is a river that was formed by the spit and blood from Fenris' jaws.

Fenris has two sons, Hati and Sköll, born to a Jötun in the Iron Wood. She is not named but it is hinted that she is probably Angrboða. At Ragnarök, Hati will swallow the Moon and Sköll the Sun.

After Angrboða bore Fenris, Hel, and Jörmungand Odin heard a terrible prophecy about the three, so he sent the gods to bring the children to him. Hel he sent to the underworld, Jörmungand he threw into the sea, but Fenris he kept so he could keep a close eye on him. Tyr was the only god courageous enough to feed the great wolf. Fenris grew rapidly every day, and the gods feared him, so they decided to trick him and bind him. Odin commissioned three chains from the dwarves: Leyding, Drómi, and Gleipnir. The gods brought Leyding to Fenris and goaded him into testing his strength, which he easily broke. Then they brought him Drómi and told him that if he broke it, he would achieve great fame. Fenris was reluctant but risked being bound for a chance at fame. After some effort, he broke it as well. The third and strongest fetter was made by dwarves in Svartálfaheim using six magical ingredients: the footfalls of a cat, the roots of a mountain, the beard of a woman, the sinews of a bear, the breath of a fish and the spittle of a bird.

Once Gleipnir was created the gods took Fenris to the island Lyngvi on the lake Ámsvartnir. There they showed him a frail-looking silken fetter and asked him to put it on as a test of his courage. Sensing a trap, Fenris asked for one of the gods to put their hand in his mouth as a pledge of good faith. All the gods refused, but eventually Tyr stepped forward and placed his right hand in Fenris' mouth. Gleipnir was placed upon Fenris and he could not break it. The gods refused to remove the binding, so Fenris bit off Tyr's hand. With Fenris finally bound, the gods thrust a sword through his jaws, pinning them shut. They then attached a magical cord called Gelgja to Gleipnir and tied the other end to a rune stone called Þviti.

When his sons swallow the sun and moon, the earth will quake and all bindings will snap, and Fenris will be free. He and Jörmungand will arrive on the field Vigriðr at Ragnarök, and Fenris will swallow Odin. Then Odin's son Viðarr will avenge him and slay Fenris.

Forseti: The son of Baldr and Nanna, he is the Aesir god of justice and reconciliation. In Old Norse his name means "the presiding one" and he stills all strife and conflict. He holds court in his home Glitnir, which means "shining", and all who come before him leave reconciled and at peace. Forseti is a great reconciler and would be a wise choice to call on for help in matters of court or law.

Freya: The Vanir goddess of fertility, love, Seiðr and war. In Old Norse her name means "Lady", which may be more of a title than her actual name. Some of her other names are Gefn, Hörn, Sýr, Vanadís and Valfreyja. She is the daughter of Njorð and Nerthus who represents Mother Earth. Her twin brother is Frey.

Freya is the leader of the Valkyries and has the first choice of those slain in battle. She will usually pick warriors who were protectors of women and children and leave the berserkers for Odin. Her hall, Sessrúmnir ("filled with many seats") which is the equivalent to Odin's Valhöll, is on the field called Fólkvangr ("field of warriors"). She has had many lovers but is married to Óðr and they have two daughters named Hnoss and Gersimi. He is often traveling and she weeps red gold or amber when he is away.

In one of her travels she came upon Brísingamen, the most beautiful necklace ever made. This necklace was created by four dwarves named Dvalin, Álfrík, Berlingr and Ger. Freya traded a night of passion with each dwarf in exchange for it; this is not to say Freya is a prostitute. She simply knows how to get what she wants and has no qualms about it.

Freya rides a chariot pulled by two giant cats when she travels the Nine Worlds. She also has the ability to put on a feathered cloak and shapeshift into a hawk to fly through the worlds. In battle, she will ride her boar Hildisvini ("battle pig"). She is a master of Seiðr magic and has taught Odin its secrets. Freya is an excellent goddess to call on in matters of love, protection in battle, or to learn the art of Seiðr. Her rune is Fehu.

Frey: The Vanir god of fertility, prosperity, sunshine and virility, he and his father were traded to the Aesir in order to end the Aesir-Vanir war. In Old Norse his name means "Lord", which may be more of a title than an actual name. He is also known as Ing and Yngvi. His twin sister is Freya. He was so loved by the gods that they gave him

Ljóssálfheim, the world of the elves, as a teething gift. Frey has the ability to bestow pleasure and peace (Wunjo) on those asking for his assistance. He presides over the weather and sunshine so he would be wise to call upon for a good harvest (Jera).

One day he sat on Odin's throne Hliðskjálf, and looked into Jötunheim where he saw the giantess Gerðr, Gymir's daughter. He fell in love at first sight and became lovesick without her, so he sent his messenger Skírnir, armed with Frey's magical sword which can fight by itself, to arrange a marriage for him. Skírnir was able to arrange the marriage at the cost of Frey's sword. After he lost his sword, he armed himself with the antler from a stag.

Frey is often seen with his dwarven-made boar Gullinbursti "golden-bristle", and his attendants Skírnir, Byggvir and Beyla. Due to the loss of his sword, he will fall to Surt's blade at Ragnarök. His rune is Ingwaz.

Frigg: Odin's wife and the Queen of Asgard, she is a goddess of marriage and of the hearth. She is known as the "Foremost among the Goddesses" and "Lady of the Aesir". In Old Norse her name means, "wife" or "beloved one". Frigg and Odin are the parents of Baldr, who was slain by Höðr. She is the highest goddess of the Aesir and has twelve handmaidens attending to her. Her hall in Asgard is called Fensalir "marsh halls" and her rune is Berkano, the Birch Goddess.

Frigg's Handmaidens

Fulla: Frigg's sister, she may also be named Volla or Abundantia. In Old Norse her name means "bountiful" and she is the virgin goddess of abundance and harvest. She is Frigg's primary confidant and keeps all of Frigg's secrets.

Eir: Aesir Goddess of medical skill and healing. In Old Norse her name means "help" or "mercy". She is the protector from disease and pestilence. Men and women would make a blót to her every summer and would be safe from all illnesses. Eir is also listed as one of the Valkyries with the ability to raise the dead.

Gefjon: Associated with harvest and plowing, she is a virgin goddess and all women who die a virgin become her attendants. Gefjon has the ability to see into the future and make prophecies. In Old Norse her name means "she who gives happiness".

Gná: Frigg's messenger who travels the Nine Worlds on her flying horse Hófvarpnir, "hoof kicker". Gná is called the goddess of fullness.

Sága: The goddess of books and histories, she is a seeress who drinks from golden cups with Odin at Sökkvabekkr, "sunken hall". In Old Norse her name means "to see".

Hlín: In Old Norse her name means "protector". Frigg sends her out to protect her chosen from danger. Hlín may very well be another Valkyrie.

Lofn: In Old Norse her name means "comforter" and she is able to reunite lovers who have been separated or forbidden to be married.

Sjöfn: The goddess of affection and love, Sjöfn has a natural counseling ability to repair any rifts between lovers.

Snotra: A goddess associated with wisdom, courtesy, and hospitality; in Old Norse her name means "clever". She is able to assist those who seek her advice on things unknown.

Syn: The shield maiden who guards the door to Fensalir, Frigg's hall, she can be called upon for defense in legal matters.

Vár: A goddess of oaths and agreements (including marriage vows), in Old Norse her name means "pledge". She will oversee and bless any oath taken in her name, but if it is broken she will punish the oathbreaker severely.

Vör: A goddess associated with wisdom and divination, her name means "the careful one". She is a Valkyrie who will seek out any information asked of her, no matter how secret.

Hel: Goddess of the Underworld, the half-corpse/half-living daughter of Loki and Angrboða. After learning that Hel and her two siblings (Fenris and Jörmungand) were being raised in Jötunheim, and fearing the prophecies about them, the gods took action. They bound Fenris, threw Jörmungand into the sea, and threw Hel into the underworld where she became the Goddess of Death. In this realm, Hel has a hall called Éljúðnir where she feeds the dead with a dish called Hunger and a knife called Famine. Hel's job, as the Goddess of Death, is to house the souls that die of sickness or old age.

Heimdall: Warder of the Gods, he stands watch on the Gjallar or Bifröst (Rainbow) Bridge until the end of days, Ragnarök. When the end comes he will sound the massive Gjallarhorn, alerting the gods and all living things through the Nine Worlds. Heimdall is Odin's son and he has nine mothers. There is some discrepancy as to their identity; some scholars say his mothers are Aegir's daughters and others claim they are a group of giantesses named Gjálp, Greip, Eistla, Eyrgjafa, Úlfrún, Angeya, Imðr, Atla and Járnsaxa.

Heimdall requires less sleep than a bird and can see in day or night for a distance over one hundred leagues. He sacrificed one of his ears to Mimir's well to be able to hear grass grow and wool as it grows on a sheep. His most defining features are his golden teeth that flash in the sunlight. When he wandered the world as a mortal man named Rig, he fathered the three classes of man (Thrall, Carl, and Earl). He is well versed in the runes and imparted that knowledge to the Earl class. Heimdall is gifted with the ability to see things unseen and predict the future, but he cannot change it. He and Loki will slay each other at Ragnarök.

Hermóðr: A son of Odin, or another name for him. Rode to Hel on Sleipnir to ask for Baldr's release.

Hoenir: One of Odin's brothers, also known as Vé, who gave Mankind hearing, speech, and sight.

Hoðr: The blind son of Odin and Frigg. He was tricked by Loki into throwing a mistletoe tipped weapon at his brother Baldr, causing his death.

Iðunn: The goddess of youth and rejuvenation, her name means "the rejuvenating one" or "ever young". She is the keeper of the golden apples which the gods eat to stay forever young and healthy. The apples are kept in an ash box, and when one is eaten, another appears. Iðunn is the maiden of eternal life and without her presence or her magical apples, the gods would wither and die.

Jörmungand: The Midgard Serpent, born to Loki and Angrboða. Odin, hearing a terrible prophecy, cast the Serpent into the sea where it grew so large that it surrounded Midgard and swallowed its own tail. At Ragnarök, it will battle Thor. In this epic battle, Thor will slay Jörmungand, but in turn will succumb to its poison after he takes nine steps.

Loki: By far the most infamous God in the entire Norse pantheon, Loki is called "the trickster", "wolf's father", "son of Laufey", Lopt, and Hveðrung. He is the son of the Jötnar Fárbauti and Laufey. Loki's brothers are Helblindi and Býleist. In some literature, Helblindi is a sea-giant, and Býleist is a storm-giant who resides in Jötunheim.

Loki is the consort of Angrboða and created three children with her: the Fenris wolf, Jörmungand the Midgard serpent, and Hel the ruler of the underworld. Through shapeshifting magic Loki changed himself into a mare and by the stallion Svaðilfari, bore Odin's eight-legged steed Sleipnir. Loki also married the Aesir goddess Sigyn and had two human sons: Narvi and Váli. After a heated argument with the gods, the Aesir changed Narvi into a wolf and he killed Váli. They then used Váli's entrails to bind Loki to a rock in a cave within the kettle-grove. There he waits until Ragnarök. Sigyn sits by his side and collects poison that drips from a snake Skaði hung above Loki's face.

Loki is both a helper and a bane to the Gods. He helped retrieve Thor's hammer from Thrym, and he traveled with Odin and Thor on many adventures and is Odin's blood brother. In a fit of jealousy, he devised a way to have the blind god Höðr slay Baldr, Odin and Frigg's most cherished son. Loki also cut off Sif's hair and stole Freya's Brisingamen.

Loki is a master of shapeshifting and Seiðr. He is extremely helpful in situations where persuasive speech is required. Some literature lists Berkano as his rune, while others claim it to be Kenaz. At Ragnarök he will break free and steer Naglfari ("the ship of the dead") from Hel loaded with shades ready for battle, where he and Heimdall will slay each other.

Mímir: Odin's uncle and guardian of Mímirsbrunnr, the Well of Wisdom.

Nát: Her name means night in Old Norse. She is the daughter of Mímir and the mother to Frigg and Njörd.

Njorð: He is originally a Vanir god of ships, wind, wealth and crop fertility. He is often called "The Sinless God", "Prince of Men" and "He who is without Malice". The patron of ships and sailors, he is the father of Frey and Freya by his Vanir sister Nerthus. Njorð lives in a bright, high-timbered temple by the sea in Nóatún where he can control the wind and sea. Those who faithfully seek his aid have been granted land and valuables.

To end the Aesir-Vanir war, he and his son, Frey were traded as hostages to the Aesir in exchange for Mímir and Hoenir. While in Asgard, he was briefly married to Skaði. Their marriage fell apart quickly because neither could live comfortably in the other's environment—Skaði was only comfortable in the snow-capped mountains of Þrymheim and Njorð could only live by the sea in Nóatún. After Ragnarök, he will be one of the few gods fated to survive, and he will return home to Vanaheim.

Norns: There are many Norns, or Fates, in Norse mythology; some are Aesir, others are Elves, Dwarves and Jötnar. Their job is to come to children as they are born to weave their thread of fate into the Web of Wyrd. The main Norns are three Jötun sisters: Urðr (past), Verðandi (present), and Skuld (future). At Urðarbrunnr (the Well of

Wyrd) they weave the Web of Wyrd which is the tapestry of the fates of every living thing. It is written that they arrived during the Golden Age of the Aesir Gods.

Odin: The All-Father and progenitor of the Aesir. He has over two hundred names (or *heiti*), including: All-Father, Hár, "Father of Victory", "Father of the Slain", ValFather, Ygg, Wodan, Wotan and Far-wanderer. He is the God of battle, victory, death, wisdom, magic, the runes and the Wild Hunt. He is the son of the giantess Bestla and Búr. Odin and his brothers Vili and Vé slew the ancient giant Ymir and used his body to create six of the Nine Worlds. He and his brothers are credited with creating the primordial man and woman, Ask and Embla.

Odin sacrificed himself in order to gain runic knowledge. He hung from Yggdrasill, the World tree, for nine days and nights, pierced by his own spear. He hung without food or water, and at the end of his ordeal he had gained the knowledge of the runes. At the Well of Wisdom, he sacrificed his eye in order to be allowed to drink from it. The Óðroerir gave him mastery of the rune songs and knowledge of the past, present, and future. Odin also has two ravens, Huginn and Muninn (thought and memory) through whose eyes he sees.

Odin is married to Frigg and he fathered Baldr and Höðr. By the earth goddess Fjörgyn (Jord) he fathered Thor. By the Jötun Griðr he fathered Viðarr, by the Jötun Gunnlöð he fathered Bragi, and by the Jötun Rind he fathered Váli. When Odin rides his eight legged steed, Sleipnir, through the Nine Worlds he is flanked by his wolves, Geri and Freki, and his two ravens. He is armed with his spear, Gungnir, which never misses its target.

Odin resides in one of his three abodes in Asgard: Glaðsheim, Valaskjálf, or Valhöll. Glaðsheim is Asgard's town hall where twelve judges preside over the world's affairs. Valaskjálf is Odin's palace built out of silver. Inside it is his elevated throne called Hliðskjálf. When he sits upon it he can see into any of the Nine Worlds. His other palace is Valhöll or Valhalla. It has 540 gates and the walls are lined with gold, spears, and all forms of armor.

Odin sends his Valkyries (among them Geirahöð, Geiravör, Geirdriful, Geirönul, Geirskögul, Göll, Guðr, Gunnr, Herfjötur, Hildr, Hlökk, Hrist, Mist, Ráðgríð, Randgríð, Reginleif, Skeggjöld, Skögull, Skuld, Þrima, and Þruðr) to fields of battle to recruit the honorable warriors who have been slain in battle. The lucky who are granted entrance to Valhalla are called the Einherjar. Their job is to practice their battle skills until Ragnarök where they will assist the Gods in the final battle. Odin's rune is Ansuz and his sign is the Valknut.

Sif: Thor's wife, known for her long golden hair. She is the mother of Ullr, Þruðr, and Lóriði. She is associated with the fields of grain and crop fertility. As a prank, Loki sheared off all of her hair while she slept, but Thor caught him and threatened to kill him if he did not do something to fix it, so Loki went to the Dwarves and had a golden wig made that grew as if it was her own hair. The same Dwarves (the Sons of Ívaldi) created Gungnir (Odin's spear), Gullinbursti (Frey's boar), Skíðblaðnir (Frey's ship), Draupnir (Odin's ring), and Mjöllnir (Thor's hammer).

Sigyn: She is a goddess and wife of Loki. In Old Norse her name means "victorious girlfriend". She and Loki have two sons, Váli and Narvi. After a heated argument with Loki, Odin changed Váli into a wolf and he killed Narvi. Odin then used his entrails to bind Loki to a stone and Skaði hung a snake over his face. Sigyn chose to stay by his side, where she catches the snake's venom in a bowl. When it becomes full she leaves his side to pour out the venom. In her brief absence the snake drips venom onto Loki's face, making him writhe and scream out in pain, and causing earthquakes. Sigyn can be seen as a loving wife who stays by her husband through the absolute worst of times.

Skaði: A Jötun huntress who lives in the snow-covered mountains of Þrymheim. She is called "Ski Goddess" or "Ski Lady", and she is known for her bow-hunting and survival skills. In Old Norse her name means "harm". She is the daughter of the Jötun Þjazi, who was slain by the Aesir. When she learned of her father's death, she equipped herself for war and traveled to Asgard to demand wergild (a reparation for the unlawful murder of a family member). The Aesir offered her a three-part wergild. First, she was allowed to choose a husband amongst them, but could only see their feet. Hoping to pick Baldr, she chose the owner of the most handsome feet, but to her dismay, those feet belonged to Njorð. The second part of her wergild was that the gods had to make her laugh, as she had experienced no happiness or joy since her father's death. Hearing this, Loki tied a rope to his testicles and tied the other end to a goat's beard. The goat thrashed and screeched and dragged Loki all through Asgard. Loki eventually returned and collapsed into her lap and she burst into laughter. Lastly, Odin took Þjazi's eyes and hurled them into the heavens where they became stars.

Ages later, at Aegir's feast, Loki was in a heated argument with the gods. When Skaði tried to interject, Loki told her that he was the first Aesir to strike her father. Skaði teold him that one day he would be bound to a rock by the entrails of his son. Loki scoffed at this prophecy and said that she used her mouth for nicer things when they slept together. Skaði was so infuriated and scorned by his words that when Loki was bound, she hung a poisonous snake over his face that dripped acidic venom into his face until Ragnarök

Surt: The oldest Jötun and ruler of Múspelheim, his name means "black" in Old Norse. He is a major figure in Ragnarök, because he will come from Múspelheim in the South leading an army. With his shining sword he will slay Frey, and the fires of Múspelheim will consume the worlds. Until then, he guards the entrance to Múspelheim.

Thor: The Aesir god of thunder and lightning and the protector of Mankind, he is called upon for strength, healing, fertility, protection and hallowing. Thor is called many different names such as: Hlórrið, "Serpent's slayer", "Reiner of goats", "Savior of Men", "Son of Jorð", "Fjörgyn's first born", Vingþor, and Redbeard, just to name a few.

Thor is the son of Odin and the earth goddess Fjörgyn or Jorð. He is the husband to Sif and the consort of the giantess Járnsaxa. He is the father of Þrúðr, Magni, and Móði. Thor rides a chariot pulled by two goats, Tanngrisnir and Tanngnióstr. His home is called Þrúðheim, which means "Land of Strength".

Thor keeps Midgard safe from invading giants with his hammer Mjöllnir. Most Ásatrúar wear a wooden or bronze pendant of Thor's hammer as a sign of his strength and protection in their lives. Thor is the strongest of the gods because of his lineage of Odin and Fjörgyn/ Jorð. Some literature lists her as a Jötun, while others say she represents the earth itself, which would account for his unnatural strength. He is the second most popular god, next to Odin. At Ragnarök, he will fight and slay Jörmungand only to die nine steps later from the serpent's poison. Thor's rune is Thurisaz, which is used as both protection and a hex rune.

Tyr: The God of justice, honor, victory, and war, he embodies the concepts of self-sacrifice and right action. In order to bind Fenris, he placed his right hand in the wolf's mouth and promised an oath that if Fenris could not break the magical ribbon Gleipnir, he would let him loose. When Gleipnir held and Tyr broke his oath, Fenris bit off his hand. Tyr sacrificed his hand and broke his oath for the greater good, because binding Fenris kept the Gods safe until Ragnarök. As a result of his loss, he is called "leavings of the wolf". At Ragnarök he is fated to battle Garm, the guard dog of Hel. When their fight is over, neither one will live.

In Old Norse, Tyr means "God" or "Heavenly Being". He may be the original Sky God that created the heavens. His father is the giant Hymir, and his grandmother is a Jötun with nine heads. Although his father and grandmother are Jötun folk, Tyr is listed as amongst the Aesir gods. Tyr has always been identified with the Teiwaz rune.

Ullr: Son of Sif and Egill and brother to Óðr, Freya's husband. He is the Aesir god of archery and the winter hunt.

Váli: Not to be confused with Loki's son by the same name, this is the son of Odin and Rind. He was conceived for the sole purpose to avenge his brother Baldr's death. He may also be known as Rán. He and his brother Viðarr will survive Ragnarök.

Viðarr: Odin's son with Gríðr who will avenge his father's death by slaying Fenris at Ragnarök.

Vili and Vé: The sons of Bestla and Búr and brothers to Odin. In Old Norse Vili means "will" and Vé means "holiness". They, along with Odin, are credited with creating the primordial man and woman, Ask and Embla. Odin gave them soul, Vili gave them intelligence, and Vé gave them senses and good color.

Wights

We use the term *wight* (the Old English version of the Old Norse *vaettir*) to classify beings that are lesser deities compared to the Aesir, Vanir, or Rökkr Gods. Some folk pray to them for help on a much smaller scale. Wights such as Niðhogg or Ratatosk serve specific purpose in their worlds and usually refuse to communicate or provide any assistance to us. They are not necessarily harmful if encountered, but it would be wise to leave them alone.

Disir: The spirits of our female ancestors that assist us in smaller things like finding our lost car keys. They are almost always helpful, but a few have been known to be malicious depending on how they were treated in life.

Eggþér: A giant called "Sword Breaker", he is the keeper of Volund's sword of revenge. Eggþér sits in Jötunheim and watches Asgard for any sign of their attack. At Ragnarök he will strike his harp warning Jötunheim of battle.

Garm: The blood-stained Hel-hound that guards Hel's gate. Many authors create parallels between Garm and Fenris. He is chained in a cave called Gnipahellir, and when Ragnarök comes his chains will break and he will run free.

Guardians of the four directions: These four dwarves hold up Ymir's skull and protect the four directions: Norðri (North), Suðri (South), Austri (East), and Vestri (West).

Harts of Yggdrasill: Four deer chew on the leaves of Yggdrasill. These deer were once dwarves named Dáin, Dvalin, Duneyr, Dýraþrór.

Hraesvelg: A wind-giant in eagle form that sits atop Yggdrasill, it is called "corpse-gulper" and controls the wind with its wings.

Niðhögg: The dragon that resides in the Nitha Fells ("Dark Fells") or Náströnd ("the Strand of the Dead"), the area between Niflheim and Helheim. She and her serpent brood, named Góinn, Móinn, Grábak, Ófnir, Grafvolluð and Sváfnir, drink the blood of the slain and devour the corpses of the dead. She is called "malice striker" or "dastardly striker", and she torments and tortures oathbreakers who are unlucky enough to end up in the lower recesses of Hel and Niflheim. Niðhögg gnaws on one of the three roots of Yggdrasill that is exposed in Niflheim. When she is not busy, she sends insults to Hraesvelg via Ratatosk. At Ragnarök, she will rise from Nitha Fells with corpses in her mouth.

Ratatosk: The squirrel that runs up and down the World Tree carrying messages and insults between Niðhogg and Hraesvelg, its name means either "rat tusk" or "teeth that find". It generally will not communicate with us.

Yggdrasill and the Nine Worlds

Yggdrasill, the World Tree, lies at the center of the universe inside Ginnungagap. It has three roots that drink from three sacred wells: the Well of Urðabrunnr in Asgard, the Well of Mímirsbrunnr in Jötunheim, and the Spring of Hvergelmir in Niflheim. The holy Norns come to Urðabrunnr (the Well of Wyrd) daily to weave our fates into the Web of Wyrd. They also keep Yggdrasill healthy by pouring water from the well over the branches and leaves to reverse the damage done by its denizens. Mímirsbrunnr (the Well of Wisdom) holds Odin's eye that he sacrificed for a drink from it which in turn granted him Divine wisdom. Niðhögg guards the spring of Hraesvelg; she also chews on Yggdrasill's roots above.

Many creatures live on the world tree, such as Hraesvelg, an Etin in eagle form, who controls the winds from atop Yggdrasill. Hraesvelg employs a squirrel named Ratatosk to send threatening messages down the tree to Niðhögg. Four dwarfs' spirits in the form of harts prune the highest boughs; their names are Dáinn, Dvalinn, Duneyrr, and Duraþrór.

In the beginning of time, Ginnungagap Mánifested an Ash seed and gestated it into the World Tree to one day hold up the nine worlds: Asgard, Midgard, Vanaheim, Jötunheim, Múspellheim, Niflheim, Ljossalfheim, Svartalfheim, and Hel. Each world is connected to Midgard by a section of the Bifröst Bridge. The Gods and runesters who have unlocked the secrets of the runes use it to travel throughout the worlds.

ଔ **Asgard,** home to the Aesir Gods, fashioned from Ymir's neck bones, sits at the highest point of Yggdrasill. All the Aesir Gods have lavish halls here. Odin and his wife Frigg hold court daily at Urðabrunnr to determine the fates of Gods and men. At night, Odin feasts with the Einherjar in Valhöll, the hall of fallen warriors.

ଔ **Midgard,** home to mankind, created from Ymir's eyelashes, lies at the middle of the World Tree. Midgard is often referred to as "Middle Earth". It is surrounded by a vast ocean in which Jörmungand lives. Odin threw it there as a baby and it grew so large that it encircled Midgard and swallowed its own tail. Jormungand lies in wait until Ragnarök when it will rise from the ocean and help Loki, Surt, and Fenris destroy Mankind.

ଔ **Vanaheim,** home to the Vanir Gods, fashioned from Ymir's pelvis, lies to the west of Midgard. Vanaheim is the original home of Frey, Freya, and Njörð. The Vanir Gods traded Njörð and Frey for Hoenir and Mimir for Kvasir to the Aesir to end the Aesir/Vanir war. The Vanir Gods are known for fertility (Frey), wisdom (Njord), and Seiðr (Freya).

ଔ **Jötunheim,** home to the Jötnar, created from Ymir's back, lies to the east of Midgard. Jötunheim is home to Angrboða, the first wife of Loki. It is ruled by King Þrym who will lead his army against Odin and the Einherjar at Ragnarök. The Jötun are powerful giants known for their strength and shape-shifting abilities.

℞ **Múspellheim**, the world of fire, heat, and light, was the first world created by Ginnungagap. It lies to the South of Midgard and is ruled by Surt. It is populated by fire giants who will follow Surt into final battle at Ragnarök. Their numbers are so vast that they will collapse the Bifröst Bridge when they march.

℞ **Niflheim**, the world of ice, cold and darkness was the second and final primordial world created by Ginnungagap. It lies to the north of Midgard and is populated by frost giants. Its lower levels are home to Hel and the dead souls under her care.

℞ **Ljossálfheim**, home to the Elves, is above Midgard on Yggdrasill. The Gods of the Aesir cherished Frey so much that they gave him Ljossálfheim as a teething gift.

℞ **Svartálfheim**, home to the Dwarves (also known as Dark Elves or Dökkálfar), was created from Ymir's lower spine and attached to Yggdrasill below Midgard. The Dwarves live underground and craft magical items for the Gods such as Gleipnir the binding of Fenris, Frey's boar, Brísingamen and Sif's golden hair.

℞ **Hel** or **Niflhel** is the final resting place for the souls of those who died of sickness or old age. Loki's daughter Hel was cast into the lower regions of Niflheim as a child. There she built her kingdom and presides over the souls from her hall Éljúðnir. Hel is a realm unto itself. Even though it lies in the bottom most level of Niflheim, it is considered to be a separate world.

The Soul

Our Nordic ancestors had a complex concept of what made up the soul. There are many books on this subject that delve into the inner workings of the soul in great detail. This section is meant to only provide you with a basic introduction to the six elements we feel are most important.

ℛ *Lík or Líkamr* is our physical body that maintains our vital health functions and also acts as a conduit for our magical energy. We, as Odinists, must keep our *Lík* healthy and hale in order to ensure that the other soul elements can perform correctly. If we do not eat correctly, exercise, and meditate, our bodies will become ill and break down, and so will the other soul elements.

ℛ *Hamr* is our astral body. It is the same shape and size as our *Lík*. Odinists who learn Vitki can manipulate their *hamr* into different animal forms while out of their body or world walking. In Old Norse literature, shamans were able to leave their *Lík* using their *hamr* and shapeshift into an animal form to do battle with their energy.

ℛ *Hugr* is our conscious thought and will. Once we learn how to harness its energy, we can project our will out into the world.

ℛ *Munr or Minni* is our individual as well as ancestral memory or collective unconscious. Our memory of past events lies on the top layer of our mind. When we meditate we can open pathways to a warehouse of ancestral memories. Within these memories, Odin has left us a blueprint on unlocking the secret of the runes.

ℛ *Fylgja* is our "fetch" or follower spirit. We have an animal-*fylgja* and a human-*fylgja* or *Valkyrja*. Our animal-*fylgja* takes the form of the animal that represents us best. Masters of Vitki can transfer their *hugr* into their animal-*fylgja* and travel the nine worlds. The *Valkyrja* is akin to a guardian ancestor spirit, and is passed on from generation to generation. We cannot control this fetch, but can rely on him/her for advice and help in time of need.

ରେ *Hamingja* is the most complex of the six soul elements. It is comprised of our luck and good/bad fortune and our shapeshifting ability, and is the well of energy that our *fylgja* draws from. Our *hamingja* is passed down from our ancestors, giving us either a boon or a curse. If the previous owner was unlucky in life, we will have a black cloud looming over us until we learn to change our fortune through actions and rituals. If we have exceptionally good *hamingja*, we can lend it to others in their time of need when they need good luck.

The Afterlife

Our Ancestors passed down to us, through written and oral tradition, their beliefs about where our *hamr* went when our *Lík* died. Our destination depended on how we lived and what caused our *Lík* to die. If you lived a righteous life and died in the service of the gods by protecting the Old Ways, your *Hamr* would be destined for Gimlé or Andlang, the highest of the heavens where the survivors of Ragnarök live.

If you were a warrior who lived a virtuous life and died in battle, your *Hamr* would be destined for Valhöll to become one of the Einherjar. If you lived a virtuous life and died protecting women, children, the elderly, or animals, your *Hamr* would be destined for Folkvang, Freya's hall.

If you were neither a warrior or a protector and died of sickness or old age, your *Hamr* would probably be destined for the upper levels of Hel. This part of Hel is not a place of punishment, but one of quiet reflection. This is where Baldr resides until Ragnarök.

If you lived a dishonorable life or were an oath breaker, your only destination would be the lowest levels of Hel where you would be tormented by Nidhögg.

The Nine Noble Virtues

The Nine Noble Virtues are a set of guidelines for us to live by. They are based on virtues described in the Poetic Edda, the Icelandic Sagas and other historical Norse texts. As Odinists, we accept these virtues as one of the cornerstones of our faith. In order to stay true to the Old Ways, we must strive to live according to them.

1. Strength

The virtue of strength not only encompasses physical prowress, but emotional and mental as well. We must identify our weaknesses and strive to overcome them.

2. Courage

We must be courageous in the face of adversity. We must identify what the right action is and have courage to take it, even in the face of fear.

3. Joy

As a folk, we are not constrained to a dogma that requires us to punish ourselves when we experience joy or satisfaction. We embrace and celebrate our achievements and take pride in them and the accomplishments of our folk.

4. Honor

Our word is our bond that must never be broken. Never take an oath unless you are sure you can fulfill it. It takes many actions to build your honor, but a single dishonorable action will destroy it.

5. Freedom

We must strive to become self-sufficient and self-reliant as a folk. We must identify the chains that bind us to negativity and poisonous things, people, ideas, etc. Once we do, we must break them in order to continue on a path of righteousness.

6. Kinship

Man and woman were not meant to live a life of isolation and solitude. Our ancestors lived in tight communities that provided safety, security, and a division of labor. Seek out other kinfolk and forge new friendships to keep the Old Ways alive.

7. Realism

We must have a realistic outlook on life. We cannot expect positive outcomes by only implementing hope and blind faith. We must put forth effort to make a positive change. Faith without work is dead. We must be realistic in our prayers as well; we cannot expect the Gods and Goddesses to answer frivolous or grandiose requests. Prayers for world peace or winning the lottery will go unanswered. We are where we are in life due to our actions and our Web of Wyrd. We cannot blame the Gods and Goddesses for our situation in life. If you do not like your life, *you* must take actions in order to change it.

8. Vigor

Sloth, laziness, and gluttony are unhealthy and they breed contempt amongst the folk. We as a people choose to embrace life. We do not sit back and watch it pass us by.

9. Ancestry

We must stand true to the ways, faith, Gods, and Goddesses of our ancestors. We must acknowledge our divine heritage and honor the Gods, Goddesses, and our ancestors in word and deed.

The Rede of Honor for Odinism

1. In all that you do, always consider its benefit or harm upon yourself, your children and your folk.

2. All that which you do will return to you, sooner or later, for good or for ill. Thus, strive always to do good to others, or at least strive always to be just.

3. Be honest with yourself, and with others, "This above all; to thine own self be trú."

4. Humankind, and especially your own family and folk, has the spark of divinity within it! Protect and nurture that spark.

5. Give your word sparingly and adhere to it like iron. Break no oath!

6. In life, your first trust and responsibility should always be to your own folk and people. Yet be kind and proper to others when possible.

7. What you have, hold!

8. Pass on to others only those words which you have personally verified.

9. Be honest with others and let them know that you expect honesty in return.

10. The fury of the moment plays folly with the truth; To keep one's head is a virtue.

11. Know which battles should be fought, and which battles should be avoided. Also, know when to break off a conflict. There are times when the minions of chaos are simply too strong, or when fate is absolutely unavoidable.

12. When you gain power, use it carefully and use it well.

13. Courage and honor endure forever. Their echoes remain when the mountains have crumbled to dust.

14. Pledge friendship and your services to those who are worthy! Strengthen others of your people and they will strengthen you.

15. Love and care for your family always, and have the fierceness of a wolf in their protection.

16. Honor yourself, have pride in yourself, do your best and forgive yourself when you must.

17. Try always to be above reproach in the eyes of the world.

18. Those of your people should always endeavor to settle any differences among themselves quietly and peaceably.

19. If the laws of the land are beneficial to the folk and family, they should be obeyed.

20. Have pride in yourself, your family and your folk. They are your promise for the future.

21. Do not neglect your mate and children.

22. Every one of our people should work according to the best that he/she can do, no matter how small or great. We are all in this world together, thus we must always help each other along.

23. One advances individually and collectively only by living in harmony with the natural order of the world.

24. The seeking of wisdom is a high virtue. Love of truth, honor, courage and loyalty are the hallmarks of the noble soul (Æthling).

25. Be prepared for whatever the future brings.

26. Life, with all its joys, struggles and ambiguities is to be embraced and lived to the fullest.

The Six-fold Goal

ℛ **Right** is ruled over by Tyr. It is the justice of the law shaped by the lore of our Folk, meted out with good judgment and true by those who can see the truth. This is a goal rationally sought and rationally administered—the rule of rationality and enlightenment in the world. From this our desire to see a world ruled rationally is derived.

ℛ **Wisdom** is watched over by Odin. This is the hidden lore and powers, welling up from the deepest depths of our soul and hovering high over our heads shining beyond the clouds, and leading us on into the unknown. This is the mysterious force that has the ability to hold all things together, ruled by those who can see and understand the whole. Above all, wisdom must be preserved, for in it are the wells of all memory. It and only it survives, all other parts of the whole may be regenerated. From this is derived our sense of adventure, our curiosity about the unknown, our seeking and questing character.

ℛ **Might** is wielded by Thor. In might is embodied the twofold goal of victory and defense, which both depend on pure power or might for their ultimate right. Without this pivotal goal, all others will fall into decay and be overcome by things outside truth, as indeed they have been. However, might must be ruled over by right and wisdom. There is worth in might in and of itself, for in the bodily expression of power is found the joy of victory which acts as a balm on the soul, and can be turned without or within the true man or woman—but it must find expression. From this is derived our hunger for conquests, big and small, and our great will to power.

ℛ **Harvest** is holy to the Wanes. This is the reaping of all things in the good cycles of nature, which ensures that the Folk continue to flourish in the world: that the livestock abound in good health: and that the seed is rightly planted, cut, and threshed. Harvest is the overriding need for the continuance of organic life. Harvest here includes all of the fruits of economic circles. It is the goodness of plenty, of wealth, and physical well-being. Today our society and our desire for abundance and wealth is dominated by this value system.

ᘓ **Frith** is ruled by Frey and Freya. Frith is our own word for peace. Frith is the true state of peace wherein all parts of the six-fold goal are successfully pursued and attained by society. In frith is true freedom, for frith is the state in which self-willed, self-directed growth and development can take place. Frith usually implies an absence of war but not of struggle or conflict. which must always be present on some level when true growth is taking place. In frith we do not stand still: in frith we learn how to take our flights to ever higher fields. Right/Might/Frith form ungoverned might. From frith comes our almost universal desire for peace, but if we misunderstand what this means, we can bring ourselves not peace but stagnation and death.

ᘓ **Love** is the law of life and is embodied in Frey and Freya, "the Lord and the Lady". This can be both pure powerful love, or the lust of eroticism. In it is our sense of play and pure pleasure. The stem word from which love is derived really has to do with the enjoyment of (physical) pleasure. That we all seek that as a goal in itself is natural and good, but it is not without its non-natural or spiritual sides, to be sure. In seeking pleasure we show (and more importantly experience) an unbridled lust for life itself. This deep well of desire acts from below much the same way that wisdom does from above. In fact, there is a secret bond between them. Wisdom and love hold the six goals together. Thinking about these tenets as the things always worth striving for (as far as the Folk are concerned as well as for individual true men and women in their own lives), will act as a guidepost for holding true values.

These goals were usually unspoken in the times of our ancestors, but they were always implicit in all that was done in nights of yore. These are ideas to work with. You should take these ideas and work out your own beliefs that abide by the Law of Nature.

Nine-Step Guide to Establishing an Ásatrú Group in Prison

Step 1: State your Religious preference.

Step 2: Find like-minded individuals who are interested in the Ásatrú religion.

Step 3: Contact outside organizations for information and assistance in getting your kindred started.

Step 4: Submit your "Request to Staff Member".

Step 5: While you wait for your answer, study and learn all you can about the Ásatrú religion.

Step 6: Work with the Chaplain/Administration on getting started. Order books, tapes, ritual items, and other necessities.

Step 7: Put up flyers. Let the population know that the Administration has approved the Ásatrú religion at your facility.

Step 8: Have your first meeting. Set up your kindred structure.

Step 9: If you are denied, be tenacious with repeated requests. Stonewalling is a common reaction to initial requests, so don't give up. Perseverance is a virtue!

Hopefully at this point you have done some reading and research and have decided that you wish to follow the religion and way of life called Ásatrú. This is a serious step on your part and one that you should spend some time thinking about. It will take a definite commitment on your part to learn all there is to know about the Ásatrú way of life. If you are ready to make that commitment, then read on.

STEP ONE: Upon entering the institution, you should have been asked for your "Religious Preference". If you listed yourself as Ásatrú, move on to Step Two. If you listed yourself as something other than Ásatrú, then you need to submit a "Request To Staff Member" asking that your Religious Preference be changed to Ásatrú.

STEP TWO: Take some time to talk with some of your fellow' prisoners to see if there are any like-minded individuals who are also interested in the religion of Ásatrú. Remember, there is strength in numbers.

STEP THREE: You should get into contact with an outside kindred or organization such as the Ásatrú Alliance of Independent Kindreds and let them know that you are interested in Ásatrú and want to establish a kindred. Ask them to provide whatever help and information they can. Be sure to include your chaplain's name and address so they can also contact him with a letter and information. A letter from an outside group or organization can really make a big difference when you are trying to get Ásatrú recognized where you are. Be sure to follow up with a letter of thanks and continue to update them on your progress.

STEP FOUR: Submit a "Request to Staff Member" asking that you be allowed to practice the religion of your ancestors, which is Ásatrú. Explain clearly what you are requesting. If you don't ask for something, you won't get it. Be sure to list outside sources for the administration to contact in order to verify the information you are providing. Be sure to list any other institutions in your region or state that already allow the practice of Ásatrú. This will make it harder for the administration to say "No". The following are some examples of what you should clearly request when you are just getting started.

- A place and time to study and hold classes.
- A place to conduct rituals, both inside and outdoors.
- Various ritual items to be used by kindred during rituals and class time. These are to be stored in the chapel, and are usually the property of the chapel.
- An altar and storage cabinet.
- Permission to have in your possession various religious items for personal use, such as a Thor's Hammer, medallion, rune set, headbands, etc. These must be bought by you and are to be stored in your locker.

Keep in mind that all these items must meet any policy on personal property set by the federal or state institution that you are in. These will also vary depending on the security level of the institution you are in. The important thing to keep in mind is that you must clearly show the importance and need for the things you are requesting. Explain exactly why it is needed, how it will be used, where it will be stored, and so forth. Make it easy for them to approve your request. One of the most important things you will need at this point (and one you should do some figuring on due to the costs, and huge selections) is a good selection of books, magazines and periodicals on a variety of subjects pertaining to Ásatrú. It is also a good idea to see about getting some films, tapes and any other study guides you can find.

STEP FIVE: Await your answer from the administration. Use this time to learn all you can about Ásatrú and our way of life. Share what you learn with others: let them see the knowledge you take in being put into action. Your honorable actions may spark an interest in others so that their ancestral memories are awakened and they become interested in the ways of their ancestors and the religion of Ásatrú.

STEP SIX: Hopefully, at this point, you will be allowed to begin practicing the religion and way of life called Ásatrú. You will be asked to begin working with the Chaplain and Administration to figure out what kind of funding they will be providing the new Ásatrú community with. These start-up funds should be spent on books, films, ritual items, tapes and any other items you feel you need at this time. Get the things you feel are the most important first, as you will only have a limited amount to spend. Order one copy each of the books—you can pass them around.

STEP SEVEN: Ask the Chaplain to approve you putting up flyers and letting the population know that the religion of Ásatrú has been approved. List the place and time you will be meeting. It would also be a good idea to have brochures, such as "'Some Answered Questions about the Ásatrú Religion", to give out. These are great for answering some of the most commonly asked questions about the religion of Ásatrú and are available in bulk from World Tree Publications.

STEP EIGHT: You are ready to have your first kindred meeting and there will be a lot to discuss. You will need to begin work on your kindred structure—to figure out who is willing to step up and take charge. In the section dealing with kindred structure you will find some things that have worked well for us, but you will still need to decide what is best for your own kindred, as each situation is unique. It is also a good time to start discussing the possibility of joining a recognized Alliance of Kindreds. Our kindred has been a proud member of the Ásatrú Alliance of Independent Kindreds since we were founded, and we have had a lot of help and support from their prison ministry from day one. (Their address is Ásatrú Alliance, P.O. Box 961, Payson, AZ 85547.) Official recognition by an outside organization is something you and your kindred can be proud of.

These are some things that should be dealt with in a manner that will show the administration that you are organized and will use the time and space you are given in the appropriate manner. By doing this, you are showing both the administration and your fellow prisoners that you are serious about your commitment to the religion and way of life called Ásatrú. In turn, this could help you in gaining acceptance and respect from both the staff and your fellow prisoners.

One of the things we stress in our Kindred is that we are a reflection of all that we hold to be holy. Our words and actions are being observed by people who would like nothing better than to see us fail or bring disgrace upon Ásatrú. For those of you just starting out on this path, it will be even tougher, but be strong and walk with your head held high. Keep in mind all the struggles our ancestors faced in their time. Now it is our time. May our descendants likewise be as proud of our words and actions.

In all that you do, consider its benefit or harm upon yourself,
your children, and your people.

If your request gets denied for whatever reason, your next step would be to file an administrative remedy. In the Federal system, you would start with the BP-8. Hopefully you will get some relief. If not, then you continue through to the BP-9. and up to the BP-11.

- ⚬ BP-8 asks for an informal solution.
- ⚬ BP-9 is an appeal to the warden.
- ⚬ BP-10 is an appeal to the regional director.
- ⚬ BP-11 is an appeal to the Central Director in Washington. D.C.

If you are in the state system, you will have an administrative remedy of some kind. You must start the process the same way. Sometimes the administration will make you go through this process just to justify having to come up with the extra money to support this new religious community, so it is important that you follow through and go on to the next step each time you are denied.

It is also a good idea to let an outside group in the community know of your struggle, such as newspapers, local magazines, Ásatrú related-magazines, and anyone else who is willing to print your story about getting the religion of Ásatrú recognized in your facility. Ask the community to support you by writing letters or calling the administration and voicing their opinion. Support from the outside community is always a big help in matters like these and could make a difference.

It is always important to be sure to include the necessary amount of copies in all your filings. This is a reason for rejection and could cause a delay. Be sure to include all the names, addresses, and phone numbers of outside contact sources. Be sure to explain and/or answer any questions clearly and with as brief a statement as possible. If you can keep it short and to the point, it will be easier for the administration to understand what you are asking for. Consider sending everything you mail through certified mail so you will have a record. The extra cost is worth it.

If, after you have exhausted your administrative remedy process, you are still denied the right to practice the way of life and religion called Ásatrú, then you need to consider filing a lawsuit on behalf of those interested in the religion of Ásatrú. Contact outside groups and let them know what is going on. A lawsuit could have already been filed in your region or state and you could possibly add your numbers to those lawsuits already pending. Remember that there truly is strength in numbers. Eventually, freedom of religion will once again truly mean that and your efforts will allow AsaFolk to worship in the old ways as our ancestors did. Our holy groves will once again come alive as the Old Ones are honored.

A lawsuit will perhaps be your last chance to get Ásatrú recognized within your system, so make sure you do things the right way. If you don't know civil law, don't be afraid to seek out someone who does. Ask outside groups for help. This is a battle that might take some time, so while the wheels of justice are turning, continue to study and learn. Share what you learn with others.

You can always meet with one another and discuss what you have been learning, but try not to meet in large groups or you could get labeled as a gang or terrorist group. That will make getting your religion recognized even harder. Remember you are not alone in your right to get Ásatrú recognized; the battle will rage on. Never give up, and never give in; our words and actions are keeping the old ways alive.

Inmates requesting the introduction of a new component to the Religious Sevice program (schedule, meeting time and space, religious items, and attire) must provide the chaplain with a comprehensive description of the religion or component following the attached outline for consideration at the institutional, regional, and national level. Because of the necessary review at these levels, the process may require up to 120 days for completion. The committee's recommendation will be forwarded to the Warden with a copy to the Regional Director. The Warden's decision will be communicated by the Institution chaplain.

You should have concise, comprehensive writing on the following subjects, in case such documentation is asked of you:

1) Theology and History

   A) Basic History

   B) Theology

2) Requirements for Membership

   A) Requirements

   B) Total Membership

3) Religious Practices

   A) Required Daily Observances

   B) Required Weekly Observances

   C) Required Occasional Observances

   D) Religious Holy Days

4) Religious Items

   A) Personal Religious Items

   B) Congregate Religious Items

5) Medical Prohibitions

6) Dietary Standards

7) Burial Rituals

8) Literature

   A) Sacred Writings

   B) Periodicals

   C) Resource Material

9) Organizational Structure

   A) Location of Headquarters

   B) Minister of Record/Contact Person

Runic Work

Runes wilt thou find, and rightly read,
Of wondrous weight,
Of mighty magic,
Which that dyed the dread Gods,
Which that made the holy hosts,
and were etched by Odin.

Know'st how to write, know'st how to read,
Know'st how to stain, how to understand,
Know'st how to ask, know'st how to offer,
Know'st how to supplicate, know'st how to sacrifice?

- The Havamal

The Runes

I wot that I hung on a wind-tossed tree
All of nights nine,
Wounded by spear, bespoken of Odin,
Myself to myself,
Upon that tree from which none telleth
From which roots doth rise.

Neither horn they upheld nor offered me bread;
I looked below me.
Aloud I cried,
Caught up the runes, caught them up roaring,
Thence I fell back to the ground.

-The Hávamál

Although the actual antiquity of the Runes cannot be traced through either paleontology or archaeology, it is known that they date back at least to around 250 B.C.E., with further evidence of a more ancient origin no longer existing (at least to our knowledge). The word *rune* means mystery or secret. In Old Norse and Old English it was *rún* or *rūn*, respectively; in Goðic and Old High German it was *runá*. It is understood that this word goes back to a root dealing with vocal performance, suggesting a whisper or a roar. This vocal performance relates to that which many know as a *mantra* and which our Norse ancestors called *galdr*. This skill creates a vibratory harmonic which enables the *runemál* (runester) to align their energies with the Runes themselves. By practicing the skill of *galdr*, the *runemál* will learn which tones or vibrations work best for each Rune.

The actual Runes (which are carved or painted on wood, paper, stone, clay, antler or bone) that an Odinist carries serve three basic purposes. First, they are used for divinatory purposes. This is an integral aspect of our religion, as the Odinist seeks runic wisdom concerning their daily life, inner development, and understanding of the factors involved in their present circumstances. Secondly, the Runes are used as a means of communication with the divine forces to gain an understanding of the mysteries of the universe. Finally, the runes are used during rituals to establish specific energies within the circle or on the altar. These energies are associated with either the Elementals, Wights, Disir, or with certain Gods or Goddesses.

In order for an Ásatrúar or Odinist to benefit from the esoteric aspects of the Old Ways, the Runes are a necessary tool. They are just as indispensable to an Odinist as a Bible is to a Christian. The practice of the Ásatrú/Odinist religion requires a personal set of Runes for each member of the kindred. The set should be created by the *runemál* whenever possible.

The descriptions and esoteric meanings of the Elder Futhark which follows are this kindred's interpretations and experience with them. The descriptions herein are by no means an exhaustive representation. You may discover different aspects to each rune as you work with them; however, the main aspects have been agreed upon by scholars for centuries. Each rune is a spiritual entity that, when contacted, can provide protection in battle, improve health, travel the Nine Worlds through path-working and meditation, and even attain a God-consciousness.

Icelandic Rune Poem

Sometime between the 8th and 12th centuries, two rune poems were written: "The Icelandic Rune Poem" and "The Norwegian Rune Poem". These poems correspond to 16 of the 24 Elder Futhark and a more compressed system called the Younger Futhark. Of the two poems we chose to include the "Icelandic Rune Poem" because, unlike the Norwegian, it is free from the taint of Christian influence. We present the original stanzas in old Icelandic as well as the English translation. Our ancestors would *galdr* (sing or vibrate) the stanzas when working with a specific rune. Only sixteen of the twenty-four Elder Futhark have stanzas.

Fé er frænda róg
  ok flæðar viti
  ok grafseiðs gata
  aurum fylkir.

Úr er skýja grátr
  ok skára þverrir
  ok hirðis hatr.
  umbre vísi

Þurs er kvenna kvöl
  ok kletta búi
  ok varðrúnar verr.
  Saturnus þengill.

Óss er algingautr
  ok ásgarðs jöfurr,
  ok valhallar vísi.
  Jupiter oddviti.

Reið er sitjandi sæla
  ok snúðig ferð
  ok jórs erfiði.
  iter ræsir.

Kaun er barna böl
  ok bardaga [för]
  ok holdfúa hús.
  flagella konungr.

Hagall er kaldakorn
  ok krapadrífa
  ok snáka sótt.
  grando hildingr.

Nauð er Þýjar þrá
  ok þungr kostr
  ok vássamlig verk.
  opera niflungr.

Íss er árbörkr
  ok unnar þak
  ok feigra manna fár.
  glacies jöfurr.

Ár er gumna góði
  ok gott sumar
  algróinn akr.
  annus allvaldr.

Sól er skýja skjöldr
  ok skínandi röðull
  ok ísa aldrtregi.
  rota siklingr.

Týr er einhendr áss
  ok ulfs leifar
  ok hofa hilmir.
  Mars tiggi.

Bjarkan er laufgat lim
  ok lítit tré
  ok ungsamligr viðr.
  abies buðlungr.

Maðr er manns gaman
  ok moldar auki
  ok skipa skreytir.
  homo mildingr.

Lögr er vellanda vatn
  ok viðr ketill
  ok glömmungr grund.
  lacus lofðungr.

Ýr er bendr bogi
  ok brotgjarnt járn
  ok fífu fárbauti.
  arcus ynglingr.

The Elder Futhark

First Aett
Fehu (fā-hoo)   F

Fehu is the force or energy that is created when something of worth is transferred from one person to another—which, in earlier times, was usually sheep or cattle. It can cause jealousy when hoarded or not shared among kinsfolk equally. Fehu can be used throughout the Nine Worlds in the form of knowledge. When Fehu is used properly, it can bind kinsmen together towards a common goal. In a rune casting, Fehu can represent: **The fire of creation, fertility (Freya) energy and wealth.**

Fé er frænda róg	Wealth
Ok flæðar viti	source of discord among kinsmen
Ok grafseiðs gata	and fire of the sea
Aurum fylkir	and path of the serpent

Uruz (oo-rooz)   U

Uruz is the rune of untamed strength and primordial essence embodied by the great Aurochs, the massive and extinct European buffalo. It is also the wild uncontrollable force as represented in mythology by the cosmic Bovine Auðhumla. She is the vital and untamable energy of the universe. It is raw unfiltered power, as can be seen in Fenris. It shapes and patterns energy through undomesticated organic forces. Uruz can represent a natural change that cannot be evaded, such as the change from adolescence to adulthood. It can also represent drizzling rain, a force of nature, which can be helpful or harmful depending on the situation. In Old Norse, Uruz can also mean slag. Slag is the waste material that is forced out of metal when it is forged. We can see this as the garbage is forced out of us as we become stronger by using Uruz. In a rune casting, Uruz can represent: **vital strength (force), wisdom, health, and a test of will or strength.**

Úr er skýja grátr	Shower
Ok skára þverrir	lamentation of the clouds
Ok hirðis hatr	and ruin of the hay-harvest
Umbre vísi	and abomination of the shepherd

Thurisaz (thoo-rĭ-sôz)   TH

Thurisaz is the rune of active defense. We can see this aspect in nature with the rosebush's thorn. In it we also see the power of Mjölnir, Thor's hammer. With it he defends Asgard and Midgard. The energy of Thurisaz is of great value to the Gods in their struggle to maintain order throughout the Nine Worlds. Thurisaz is a force that can break down barriers and resistance (physical, emotional, mental), but if not used properly it can cause great disaster and suffering. It also symbolizes the rune of a race of giants called the Thurses who are the enemy of the Aesir, and whom, if left unchecked by Thor, would destroy the Nine Worlds. If we meditate on this rune, we will see certain aspects of our life that can lead to our downfall if left unaddressed. In a rune casting, Thurisaz can represent: **protection, applied power (force), destruction, and regeneration.**

Þurs er kvenna kvöl	Giant
Ok kletta búi	torturer of women
Ok varðrúnar verr	and cliff-dweller
Saturnus þengill	and husband of a giantess

Ansuz (än-sooz)   A

Ansuz is Odin's rune of divine consciousness, magical potential, and mouth or spoken word. It is the medium in which ancestral power is received. It is also the rune of the magical rune-song (*galdr*). Ansuz describes the divine breath and inspiration bestowed upon Ask and Embla by Odin, Vili, and Vé. The energy of this rune is Mánifested in the inspired words of the Skald as well as the ecstatic *galdr* of the *vitki* (shaman). Ansuz is the magical potential of our folk that is handed down genetically from one generation to the next and the divine power that links us to Odin. In a rune casting, Ansuz can represent: **divine breath, word song, Odinic ecstasy, poetical and magical inspiration, numinous knowledge.**

Óss er algingautr	God
Ok ásgarðs jöfurr	aged Gautr
Ok valhallar vísi	and prince of Ásgarðr
Jupiter oddviti	and lord of Vallhalla

Raiðo (rī-thō)   R

Raiðo stands for the cosmic law of right order and the path to rightly ordered action. It embodies both the concept of the journey back to the way of right action (the path to the Gods) and that of the vehicle facilitating the journey. Raiðo is the vehicle that takes us between the worlds. In a rune casting, Raiðo can represent: **the journey, right action, cosmic order and ritual.**

Reið er sitjandi sæla	Riding
Ok snúðig ferð	joy of the horsemen
Ok jórs erfiði	and speedy journey
Iter ræsir	and toil of the steed

Kenaz (Kĕ-nôz) K

Kenaz is the torch (controlled fire) of creativity, intelligence and Mánifestation. It has the ability to shape our ideas and help us bring them into reality. Kenaz is a gift from the Gods, the spark of divinity that we are able to harness and apply towards a certain purpose. We can use it to sharpen our weapons as the forge fire, kindle passion and love, embody it as the spark of health, call upon it to give us divine inspiration, or to bring the hidden into light.

It can also mean a sore or battle wound. This type of wound usually causes death which leads to a funeral pyre. The warrior's soul would leave his/her body and enter another state of being. This ability to transfer from one state to another can be harnessed by the runester. By unlocking the mysteries of Kenaz, the runester can alter their state to travel through the nine worlds. In a rune casting, Kenaz can represent: **torch, controlled energy, ability, lust, creativity, Mánifestation.**

Kaun er barna böl	Ulcer
Ok bardaga [för]	disease fatal to children
Ok holdfúa hús	and painful spot
Flagella konungr	and abode of mortification

Gebo (gā-bō) G

Gebo is the rune of exchange and sacrifice. It is Odin's gift to us as life, form and consciousness. This gift, and the act of gift-giving, binds our folk together. In olden times, as outlined in the Hávamál, mutual gift-giving ensured for a peaceful society.

Gebo is also a rune of sacrifice. Odin sacrificed himself by hanging on Yggdrasill for nine days and nights to receive the runes. This act shows us that to receive some gifts, we must sacrifice something very valuable to us. Gebo can also be seen as a rune of sex magic. Its energy and knowledge is amplified by the exchange of power between the male/female consciousnesses. In a rune casting Gebo can represent: **gift, sacrifice, sacredness, magical force, sex magic.**

Wunjo (woon-yō)   W or V

Wunjo is the rune of harmony within the kindred or runester. It embodies the absence of strife or sorrow. Wunjo promotes fellowship and goodwill, and in turn promotes a strong bond within the kindred. It would have been an excellent rune to call upon before a battle to keep a shield wall strong. Wunjo can be used in rune magic to bind other runes together. In a rune casting, Wunjo can represent: **travel, harmony, fellowship and well-being.**

Second Aett
Hagalaz (hä-gä-lôz)   H

Hagalaz means hail. It has been said that the name is derived from the Proto-etin Hagal who was able to send frozen rain and mighty gales upon his enemies. In stories about him we can see how Hagalaz can be a protective force or a weapon. Scholars also see Hagalaz as a metaphor for catastrophic growth as well. For example, hail can kill crops and destroy the blight and disease that may be growing unchecked and unbeknownst to the farmer; so by destroying the blighted crop, hail destroys disease and brings about new growth and a chance for regeneration. We see how a sudden downturn can bestow gifts upon the strong. In a rune casting, Hagalaz can represent: **hail, cosmic seed, evolution, and cosmic pattern and framework.**

Hagall er kaldakorn	Hail
Ok krapadrífa	cold grain
Ok snáka sótt	and shower of sleet
Grando hildingr	and sickness of serpents

Nauðiz (nou-thēz) N

Nauðiz is the rune of Mánifestation through need and of deliverance through distress. It is the rune of coming into being, the law of the Norns and the kindling flame of higher consciousness. It also stands for a form of distress and what must be done to overcome it. Nauðiz can also mean shackle or bondage, and has been widely used in hexcraft. It is the resistance that can be turned into a source of energy or friction. This becomes the "need fire" that creates life, inspiration, and safety. In a rune casting, Nauðiz can represent: **need-fire, friction, resistance, distress and deliverance.**

Nauð er þýar þrá	Constraint
Ok þungr kostr	grief of the bond-maid
Ok vássamlig verk	and state of oppression
Opera niflungr	and toilsome work

Isa (ĕ-sŏ) I

Isa is the rune of ice and contraction. It usually represents lack of movement, delay, freezing cold or an ice bridge. All matter in the universe is defined by a pattern of vibration. We use vibration in Galdr magic to get the attention of specific Gods, runes or energy. If we use the correct vibration of their names (or runes) we can open a channel of communication with them.

When water freezes, its vibrational pattern changes, it slows down to an imperceptible level. When we see this in a rune cast it usually means delay of plans, or a lack of movement. It can also be a sign to move or react or else failure will occur.

Isa can also be a bridge to new destinations (physical, mental, emotional, or metaphysical). This ice bridge can create a path to a different way of thinking.

Isa must be used carefully, but when used correctly it can slow vibrations of others or situations to create a calming presence. In a rune casting, Isa can represent: **ice, stasis, ego, concentration.**

Íss er árbörkr	Ice, bark of rivers
Ok unnar þak	and roof of the wave
Ok feigra manna fár	and destruction
Glacies jöfurr	of the doomed

Jera (yâr-ä)   J or Y

Jera is the rune of the harvest and life cycle. It represents harvest time or within the time frame of a year's harvest. It is hopefully the yield of a good harvest or the rewards for the seeds of right action coming into fruition. A good harvest is dependent on the farmer (runester) sowing seeds at the right time and using the correct ingredients. If the farmer planted too early or too late or neglected water and nourishment, the crop would fail. Jera is the natural progression of the seasons throughout all realms of existence. If the crop fails this year, we must learn from our mistakes and take immediate action to prevent it from happening again. In olden times, a single failed harvest could mean starvation and death for the farmer and his/her family. If the family survived the winter, they would thank the Gods and their folk for helping them through. Their next harvest would be more carefully planned to prevent failure, for failure a second time would surely mean starvation. In a rune casting, Jera can represent: **year, harvest, consequences, and cyclical developments.**

Ár er gumna góði	Plenty
Ok got sumar	boon to men
Algróinn akr	and good summer
Annus allvaldr	and thriving crops

Eihwaz (ā-väz)   Ā or EI

Eiwaz is the vertical axis of the multiverse—the Yew column of Yggdrasill. It connects Asgard and Helheim directly and is a life sustaining force that connects life and death. Another aspect is of protection because it can also represent the Yew Bow. Eihwaz can unite opposites such as life/death, or day/night. It is considered a transformative fire within the runester that can help turn a bad situation into a better one. In a rune casting, Eiwaz can represent: **protection, Yew Bow, life/death, vertical cosmic axis.** *(Note: Some Ásatrúar attribute the following rune verse to the Anglo-Frisian rune Yr.)*

Ýr er bendr bogi	Yew
Ok brotgjarnt járn	bent bow
Ok fífu fárbauti	and brittle iron
Arcus ynglingr	and giant of the arrow

Perthro (pĕr-thrō)   P

Perthro, the lot cup or dice cup, can stand for change (good or bad) or a runester testing fate or his/her luck. Perthro is the evolutionary force of constant change in the universe. If the runester is able to harness this energy, they can influence changes around them. It is also the symbol of how Ørlög functions and how Gods and folk might discern its workings. This includes the mysteries of the Norns, Wyrd and the Well of Urðr. The mystery of divination is central to Perthro, which makes a firm understanding of this rune necessary to effective practice of rune craft. In a rune casting, Perthro can represent: **lot or dice cup, fortunate omen, change, and the Norns.**

Elhaz (el-häz)   Z

Elhaz or Algiz is a powerful and ancient rune of protection. The rune looks like a hand splayed out to ward off an attack. Elhaz translates to "elk" or "stag" which connects it to Yggdrasill through the four cosmic elk that nibble on it. The energy of Elhaz rises up and branches upward towards the Gods. Elhaz can link the runester to the path of God-consciousness. This is the rune of the unbreakable bond between the Gods and folk. This connection with the Gods provides life, protection and knowledge. In a rune casting, Elhaz can represent: **elk, protection, life, connection with the Gods.**

Sowilo (sō-wē-lō)   S

Sowilo is the sun or solar rune. It is one-half of the solar wheel and resembles a lightning bolt (energy). Sowilo spins with this energy and can protect or empower the runester. It can be the internal fire that drives us to gain God-consciousness. When Sowilo represents the sun, it can create or destroy life. It can nurture crops or it can beat down on them with scorching heat. Sowilo can be used as a dynamic connection between Asgard and Midgard. In a rune casting, Sowilo can represent: **honor, success, protection, life and transformation.**

Sól er skýja skjöldr	Sun
Ok skínandi röðull	shield of the clouds
Ok ísa aldrtegi	and shining ray
Rota siklingr	and destroyer of ice

Third Aett
Teiwaz (Tē-väz)   T

Teiwaz is a representation of the god Tyr, the Sky God and the God of Justice, self-sacrifice, order and war. Many scholars believe that Tyr was the original All-Father who created space and facilitated the creation myth. Teiwaz points up to the sky and represents the world-column (Irminsul). We can also see the scales of justice represented in Teiwaz. Tyr sacrificed his hand to Fenris to preserve Wunjo among the Aesir. In olden times, warriors would call upon Tyr before battle to ensure victory. Teiwaz is the rune of the Ásatrú warrior ethic—our honorable acts, applied to a just cause, will bring victory. This rune can be called upon for strength when times are tough. In a rune casting, Teiwaz can represent: **right action, absolute justice, victory, self-discipline, and self-sacrifice.**

Týr er einhendr áss	Týr
ok ulfs leifar	god with one hand
ok hofa hilmir	and leavings of the wolf
mars tiggi	and prince of temples

Berkano (bĕr-kä-nō)   B

Berkano is the rune of the Birch Goddess who rules over rites of passage (birth, marriage, death). It is the Maiden/Mother/Crone aspect of nature. Berkano can be called on for protection and is closely tied to Frigg. Through advanced working with this rune, the runester can use it to open a direct route to Vanaheim. In a rune casting, Berkano can represent: **rebirth, Birch Goddess, and containment.**

Bjarkan er laufgat lim	Birch
Ok lítit tré	leafy twig
Ok ungsamligr viðr	and little tree
Abies buðlungr	and fresh young shrub

Ehwaz (ĕh-väz) E

M Ehwaz is the war-horse that we rely on to be loyal to us on the battlefield. We look to its physical power to assist us on and off the battlefield. Odin's war-horse, Sleipnir, not only carries him into battle, it takes him through the nine worlds. For eons, man has had a harmonious relationship with the horse. Many great warriors were buried with their horses or saddles. Ehwaz works with our intellect to be a vehicle for change. Ehwaz is also the joyful union of marriage between a man and woman. In a rune casting, Ehwaz can represent: **fertility, trust, and marriage.**

Mannaz (män-nôz) M

M Mannaz is the rune of divine structure between the Gods and Man. It describes the genetic link (via Rig) by which we were created. Rig bred with mankind and created three classes of people (Thrall, Carl, Earl). Mannaz symbolizes our divine heritage, blood brotherhood, and our ancestry to Odin. Mannaz is the divine consciousness that must be tapped into if we are to continue on our path to understand not only the runes, but our part in the universe. In a rune casting, Mannaz can represent: **ideal man, divine link, intelligence, initiate, God-consciousness.**

Maðr er manns gaman	Man, delight of man
Ok moldar auki	and augmentation
Ok skipa skreytir	of the earth
Homo mildingr	and adorner of ships

Laguz (Lä-ġooz) L

ᚱ Laguz is the rune of the primal waters of life that flow from Hvergelmir. It is a rune of transformation between life and death. It can also be used to provide vital life force or it can drag the runester under and drown him/her. Water can be used as a means of transportation, and the runester can use Laguz as a vehicle to other worlds. Laguz can Mánifest the unknown by the runester "dragging the waters" of his/her sub-conscious. It can also be a pivotal time for the "tide" to turn in the runester's favor. In a rune casting, Laguz can represent: **vital power, travel, primal force, and water.**

Lögr er vellanda vatn	Water
Ok viðr ketill	eddying stream
Ok glömmungr grund	and broad geyser
Lacus lofðungr	and the land of the fish

Ingwaz (ĭng-väz)   Ng

Ingwaz is the rune of the god Ing—the god of land and soil. He provided farmers with fertile fields and a good harvest. This function seems to have been transferred to Frey. Ingwaz is the rune of potential Mánifestation. It is the seed that may produce fruit if the runester nurtures it correctly. It can also signify the ending of one phase (cycle) and the birth of a more fruitful one. In a rune casting Ingwaz can represent: **seed, potential energy, gestation.**

Dagaz (dä-gäz)   D

Dagaz is the rune of day, meaning the period from sunrise to sunset and sunset to sunrise. It can also represent the god Dagr, who is the embodiment of day and light. Dagaz is the cyclical process of life and time—we are born and eventually pass away into a new beginning. We can also see two Kenaz runes touching each other, which can give the runester the ability to pause the flow of time. Dagaz can also represent daybreak—a bad episode in the runester's life ending. In a rune casting Dagaz can represent: **polarity between light and dark, enlightenment, consciousness.**

Othala (ō-thä-Lä)   O

Othala is the rune of inherited property, tribal lands, and our divine ancestry. It is a sacred enclosure (physical or metaphysical) that provides us with safety, tribal identity and heritage. The Holy is separated from the profane and is empowered within the enclosure. It contains the link to our ancestors, laws and Gods, and provides for our safety and security. If our ancestral and kindred laws are followed there will be peace and freedom in our lives. Through Othala we are self-governed and can experience divine sovereignty. In a rune casting Othala can represent: **inherited power, protection, and sacred enclosure.**

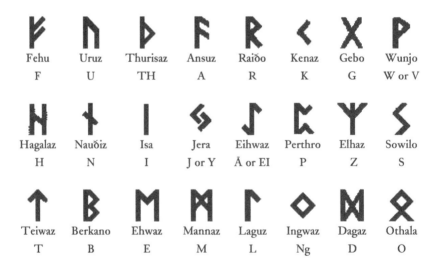

ᚠ	ᚢ	ᚦ	ᚨ	ᚱ	ᚲ	ᚷ	ᚹ
Fehu	Uruz	Thurisaz	Ansuz	Raiðo	Kenaz	Gebo	Wunjo
F	U	TH	A	R	K	G	W or V

ᚺ	ᚾ	ᛁ	ᛃ	ᛇ	ᛈ	ᛉ	ᛋ
Hagalaz	Nauðiz	Isa	Jera	Eihwaz	Perthro	Elhaz	Sowilo
H	N	I	J or Y	Ā or EI	P	Z	S

ᛏ	ᛒ	ᛖ	ᛗ	ᛚ	ᛜ	ᛞ	ᛟ
Teiwaz	Berkano	Ehwaz	Mannaz	Laguz	Ingwaz	Dagaz	Othala
T	B	E	M	L	Ng	D	O

Rune Creation Ritual

In order to be able to read the runes correctly, you must create your own set. Our ancestors carved them into wood, antler, and bone, and so must we. If you use wood, it would be best to make them from Ash or Elm. If you want to use antler or bone you can find many sources in the Midwest that sell them, or you can search fields and prairies for shed antlers or the remains of fallen deer. Whichever medium you choose, make sure there is going to be enough to cut twenty-four runes. Each rune should be thick enough to take a carving on one side, but thin enough to hold all of them in both hands. We suggest you cut your runes about 1-2 cm thick.

Once you have cut 24 blank runes, you will need the following:

- ℞ 1 awl or exacto blade
- ℞ 1 leather or cloth pouch to hold your runes
- ℞ 1 small writing brush
- ℞ Paint or ink
- ℞ 1 white altar cloth

1. Set everything on your altar, perform the hallowing rite, and say, "Odin, you hung for nine nights on Yggdrasill, wounded by your own spear. You sacrificed yourself for runic knowledge. Grant me the gift to create these runes, and read them aright."

2. With your hand, carve the runes in the air above your altar. Then say, "Holy Norns, sisters three, Urð, Verðandi, Skuld, open the runic streams for me as I strive to bring forth new life. May these runes wax and bloom and grow in power and knowledge."

3. Take the first blank rune and carve the rune Fehu against the grain. Then *galdr* (vibrate) its name three times. Feel the vibration begin from the ground and roll through your body and exit your mouth. You should expel all your breath on the exhale and visualize the rune. If you do this correctly you will feel the rune click in place.

4. With your hand, carve the rune three more times in the air while vibrating its name.

5. Take the brush and paint and carefully fill in where you carved. (Our ancestors would then fill in the rune with a drop of blood.) Then repeat step 4. Now your first rune is complete. Set it on the altar cloth to dry.

6. Repeat steps 3-5 and create the rest of your runes.

7. When the runes are dry, draw the Perthro rune on your rune bag. Then say: "Odin, bless these runes as they sleep for nine nights so that they may grow in power, grow in strength, and come to life roaring and bring to me all that I seek. Binder of the breath cord, breathe life into these runes just as you did with Ask and Embla."

8. Then *galdr*: "Ansuz, Laguz, Uruz" over your runes.

9. Place them into the bag and whisper into it: "Sleep, wax and bloom. Grow in power and come forth roaring with wisdom from all the worlds. Help me in my time of need and always answer me truthfully."

10. Seal the bag and bury it nine inches deep in the earth, away from everyone so that they will not be disturbed. If you cannot bury them, put them in a quiet dark place where they will not be disturbed.

11. Over the next nine nights, spend time reflecting on the twenty-four runes and try to gain a deeper insight on them.

12. After nine nights have passed, retrieve your runes and place them on your altar.

13. Perform the hallowing rite and call upon the Norns: "Holy Norns Urð, Verðandi, Skuld, you connect to all that has been, all that is and all that will be. May my work here be guided so that the new life brought forth will connect all that is within me and all that I can become."

14. Open the bag and say: "Come forth out of darkness into light and bring forth wisdom and power. May we be always connected through Odin who gave us both life. Grant me your runic wisdom as I strive throughout the worlds. Let us go forth this day as one. Hail Odin! Hail The Holy Norns! Hail (the secret name you gave your runes)!"

Rune Creation Ritual If Incarcerated

1. Get the following:
   - ০৪ 1 red pen/pencil
   - ০৪ 1 cup of warm water
   - ০৪ 1 roll of fresh toilet paper
   - ০৪ 1 white altar cloth or sheet of paper
   - ০৪ 1 envelope
   - ০৪ Pin or needle

2. Hallow your cell, and then place the items on your altar (or what you are temporarily using as an altar).

3. Start the toilet paper roll and discard the first nine squares. Then carefully tear off and separate twenty-four squares and place them on your altar cloth.

4. Say: "Odin, you hung for nine nights on Yggdrasill, wounded by your own spear. You sacrificed yourself for runic knowledge. Grant me the gift to create these runes and read them aright."

5. Take your first square and fold it in half from left to right. The perforated edges will be together on the right side. Fold the edge in 1/3 towards the left side, then fold it one more time. This will leave you with a 1 cm strip that is approximately 7 ½ cm long.

6. Fold it in half from top to bottom. Take the bottom and fold it up 1/3. Then take the top and fold it on top of that. This will leave you a 2 cm x 2 cm square with all rough edges tucked inside.

7. Holding the square together with your thumb and index finger, dunk it in the water. Squeeze the excess water out and smooth out the edges if need be. Place it on the altar cloth.

8. With your pen or pencil, carefully carve the first rune, Fehu. The ink will be reapplied in step 10, so don't worry about it coming in light. Then *galdr* (vibrate) its name three times. Feel the vibration begin from the ground and roll through your body and exit your mouth. You should expel all your breath on the exhale and visualize the rune. If you do this correctly, you will feel the rune click in place.

9. With your hand, carve the rune three more times in the air while vibrating its name.

10. Take your pen or pencil and carefully fill in where you carved. Then repeat step 9. Now your first rune is complete. Set it on the altar cloth to dry. If you have access to an electric fan, turn it on and point it at the rune to accelerate the drying time. If the rune is too wet, wait until dry and then reapply. Prick your finger onto each rune and let dry.

11. Repeat steps 5-10 and create the rest of your runes.

12. Draw the Pertho rune on the envelope and pad the inside of the envelope with additional toilet paper to soak up any moisture.

13. When everything has dried, say: "Odin, bless these runes as they sleep for nine nights so that they may grow in power, grow in strength, and come to life roaring and bring to me all that I seek. Binder of the breath cord, breathe life into these runes just as you did with Ask and Embla."

14. Then vibrate, "Ansuz, Laguz, Uruz" over your runes.

15. Place them into the bag and whisper into it: "Sleep, wax and bloom. Grow in power and come forth roaring with wisdom from all the worlds. Help me in my time of need and always answer me truthfully."

16. Seal the envelope and put it in a quiet dark place where it will not be disturbed.

17. After nine nights have passed, retrieve your runes and place them on your altar.

18. Perform the hallowing rite and call upon the Norns: "Holy Norns Urð, Verðandi, Skuld, you connect to all that has been, all that is and all that will be. May my work here be guided so that the new life brought forth will connect all that is within me and all that I can become."

19. Open the bag and say: "Come forth out of darkness into light and bring forth wisdom and power. May we be always connected through Odin who gave us both life. Grant me your runic wisdom as I strive throughout the worlds. Let us go forth this day as one."

Rune Casting Ritual

Once your runes are created and awoken, contemplate an appropriate question to ask the Norns. Casting runes is not parlor magic and must be taken very seriously. When casting runes, you will be asking the Norns to consult the Web of Wyrd and give you an answer. The Web of Wyrd is the tapestry of the fates of all living things. Everything you do and everyone you come in contact with will be woven into your thread. The Norns are Goddesses, and weaving this tapestry is their job; they do not want to be bothered with frivolous questions such as: "Where did I leave my keys?" Appropriate questions to ask would be: "If I choose this job, what will my future hold?" or "If I continue on this path, what will my future hold in one year's time?" The Norns will reveal first what events lead you to where you are, then your present situation and current influences will be revealed, and finally your probable future will be revealed. Remember that the Web of Wyrd is constantly in flux, and different threads are begin woven in or cut away.

Required Tools

- ☙ Your runes
- ☙ An altar cloth or white sheet
- ☙ Bowli
- ☙ Horn or cup
- ☙ Juice or mead

Set up your altar if you have one; otherwise lay out your altar cloth or white sheet in the North with your runes and bowli on it. Then hallow your space. Facing North, draw the hammer sign and say:

"Hamar í Norðri helga vé þetta ok hindra alla ilska."
Turn to the East, draw the hammer sign and say:
"Hamar í Austri helga vé þetta ok hindra alla ilska."
Turn to the South, draw the hammer sign and say:
"Hamar í Suðri helga vé þetta ok hindra alla ilska."

Turn to the West, draw the hammer sign and say:

"Hamar í Vestri helga vé þetta ok hindra alla ilska."

Return to the North and draw the hammer sign above your head, and say:

"Hamar í yfer mér helga vé þetta ok hindra alla ilska."

Draw the hammer sign on the floor and say:

"Hamar í under mér helga vé þetta ok hindra alla ilska."

Take up your runes and say: "Holy Norns Urðr, Verðandi, Skuld, empower these runes to connect with your great tapestry and show me the truthful answer to my question."

Ask your question aloud three times while shaking up the runes in your hands. Concentrate on your question and chant "Urðr, Verðandi, Skuld!" three times.

Close your eyes and say "Runes, read aright!" then cast them onto your cloth. Understand that in the moment you let them go, they dipped into the realm of the Norns, and your answer is now before you.

With your eyes still closed, assume the Elhaz stance and say: "Odin, grant me your insight to read these runes aright." Then, with your eyes still closed, pick out the first rune, which will be Urðr (past). Put it aside and pick out Verðandi (present), and finally pick out Skuld (future). Now open your eyes and look at the runes you have chosen. Raise your horn or cup and thank the Norns for their guidance. Then pour an adequate portion into the *bowli* as a sacrifice. If you are skilled in skrying, gaze into the *bowli* to divine further. When you are done, thank Odin and the Norns. Look at the rune in the Urðr position and refer to the rune section, and ask yourself how that rune fits into your past. What actions did you take that either opened a path or closed one?

Look at the rune in the Verðandi position and ask yourself those same questions. Finally, look at the rune in the Skuld position. This is what your potential future will be. Remember that your future is not static; you can always take actions to change it if you do not like what you see. If you are content with what your future will likely hold, keep on your path to fulfill it.

There are many other rune castings you can experiment with. This one is the most simple one to do and understand. When you get more comfortable with casting runes, you can choose three runes for each Norn. You will be picking three for the past, three for the present, and three for the future. This will give you much more insight into your question. You can also begin to experiment with "bright" and "murk" staves. With this method, each rune you pick up will be considered "bright" if it is face up and "murk" if it is face down. The only difference is if you chose a murk stave, it will be the negative aspect if that rune.

Rituals

Ritual: Blót, Feast, and Sumbel

Ritual, whether performed with a full understanding or not, is the means by which we as a folk continue to strengthen the Divine spark that resides within us. When we perform ritual acts, even ones we do not fully understand, we are keeping alive ancient wisdom. It is helpful that if such wisdom is preserved it will at some time be made known to a chosen few who will be able to grasp their deepest mysteries. The act of ritual also allows our sacred relics and tools to maintain their potency by continuing to be focal points for our concentration. By performing these acts we remove ourselves from the mundane world and immerse ourselves in the worlds of our Ancestral Gods.

The Importance of Blót

The Blót (Old Norse for sacrifice) is a ritual of great importance that is held on four high holy days of the year—and for many kindreds and clans, the eight lesser holy days as well. This is a time where the common folk can gather and exchange energies with the Gods and Goddesses. This is the true essence of Gebo. We are sacrificing/gifting to the Deity for something they have given us or will provide for us in the future. This exchange is essential to our way of life. We we are taught in the myths, Sagas, and the Eddas the importance of this exchange, the benefits for doing it, and the repercussion for not.

The folk today honor our Deities and ancestral spirits just as our ancestors did thousands of years ago. By performing Blót, you are keeping the old ways alive and giving anyone attending the Blót the opportunity to tap into the energy of the Gods. For it is at the Blót that we have a group of like-minded individuals who have gathered to do something that strengthens our way of life. Ásatrú is about *doing*, and the more individuals who have the spark of divinity reignited; the stronger our folk will grow.

The Blót is about reigniting that spark and making a connection that will enable you to move forward, regardless of what is placed in your path. The steps of the Blót, and the ritual tools used, allow you to make connections with the Gods and your kinfolk, both within and outside of your normal sphere. If you can truly focus on the Blót and its workings, you will gain what it is you need at that time in your life regardless of where you are on the path. With the right intent, even those stumbling about in the dark will find what they seek.

Blót Information

When you are preparing to conduct a Blót, consider the following helpful hints that will make you better prepared and ensure its power.

ᛦ Take the opportunity to explain to the participants why the Blót is being held. Try to provide lore from the Eddas and Sagas days or weeks before, and ask the participants to study and meditate upon them. The more people you have focused on your purpose or Deity, the more powerful the energy will be. The same goes for solitary Blóts—prepare, read and meditate long before you perform the Blót. There is absolutely no reason to not be prepared. Lack of preparation will bring about failure and it will be disrespectful to the Gods.

ᛦ If you are going to have someone assist you, explain what they will need to do and when, so they will be ready at the right time. It will also be helpful to explain to them why they are doing it, and the symbolism our ancestors wanted represented.

ᛦ Have the ritual tools you will need ready, including a sprig in the *bowli* for the blessing. Some kindreds set up the altar beforehand; others have members carry in the ritual items and place them on the altar. If you choose to do this, make sure everyone knows what they will be carrying.

ᛦ Have the bottle or container of mead/juice open already.

ᛦ Clean up the sacred land or area to be used beforehand and remove anything not needed.

ᛦ If a fire is to be used, have it lit beforehand or make its lighting one of the steps of the Blót. If you choose to light it during the

Blót, ensure that the person doing it has all the materials needed close at hand.

ᚳ If anyone is going to tell a story, call out the Deity's name or do a reading, be sure they have the information they need.

The Importance of Feasting

After the Blót, if at all possible, it is a time to feast. The Kindred , clan, or family all come together to share a meal and use this time to share stories and catch up on family business. We always make up a plate for ancestors who are no longer among us, and one for people who couldn't make it. There are many traditional foods you can prepare—pork, corned beef and cabbage for our Irish brothers, duck, chicken, fish, and various vegetables. This is a time of celebration, so you want your very best. However, for those on a budget or in prison, try just having a meal you can share with someone, even if it's only you and the Gods. It's sharing what you have that's important.

We always save a nice portion to sacrifice to Mother Earth for all she has given us. For some kindreds, a hero's portion is made up and set aside for that person who feels he has done something to be considered worthy. Remember, if you are brave enough to claim it, you are being judged not just by those around you but also the Gods, Goddesses, and your ancestors. So think with your head, not your stomach.

The Importance of Sumbel

Sumbel is a series of ritual drinking rounds using mead or juice in which the Gods, ancestors and heroes are honored. There may also be rounds dedicated to ritual boasting and-oath making. At the opening of Sumbel, we remove ourselves from normal space and time as we understand it and step into a time and space apart. Once this move has been made, we stand in the realm of the Gods. All words spoken over the horn are woven into our *Wyrd* and become *Örlög*. The horn is passed around the group and each person takes it, he/she becomes the focal point for that time. All eyes and ears are upon them. The speaker's words and how they are spoken have much to do with their standing in the kindred/clan. The first round is dedicated to the Gods. The speaker will raise the horn in a God's name, and then they pass it to the next speaker who will raise to a God of their choice.

After everyone has had their turn, a second round begins. In this round each speaker can hail an ancestor who has done something to be remembered for. Being able to speak well and compose verses at will are considered marks of a well-born and heroic person. The third round is for toasts, boasts and sometimes oaths. If a speaker wishes to take an oath, they should seek permission before hand, because all oaths will be tied to everyone's Wyrd in attendance.

The importance of Sumbel should never be overlooked or diminished in any way. The Sumbel is a true art form and a very important part of our folk's heritage. In this age of lost folk and meaningless lives, the Sumbel represents a path back to a true sense of pride within the folk. We are the vanguard who must preserve this and all elements of our ancient rituals.

Nine-Step Blót Format

ᚲ **Hallowing.** You are calling upon the holy forces to protect the area and the participants in the ritual. Facing North, begin the opening by saying: "Hammer in the North, Hallow and hold this holy Vé and prevent all evil from entering." Do the same to the East, South, and West, moving clockwise. You should end up back in the North, where you would ask the holy forces or a chosen deity to ward the area and keep you safe from outside influences. Various ritual tools can be used for this, and we like to do this opening in Old Norse, which can be found in the three-volume set "Rituals of Ásatrú", available from World Tree Publications.

ᚲ **Consecrate the Altar.** While drawing runes in the air over the altar with your hand or ritual tool, you can say: "I consecrate this altar and all upon it, this holy place, and all the proud Folk gathered in the name of (God/Goddess to whom the Blót is conducted)."

ᚲ **Invite the God/Goddess.** "We call upon (God/Goddess) to join us in Midgard, to come receive sacrifice that we all grow stronger in the old ways." (Find numerous names, kennings, or *heiti* by which the God/Goddess is known and use these, or have others attending the Blót call out one name each that has meaning to them.)

ᚲ **Reading.** Read a story or part of a saga or myth that explains or shows an aspect of this God/Goddess, or explains what this Blót is about and what you should be focusing on.

ᚲ **Charge Horn.** Hold the mead-filled horn up high, asking the God/Goddess to fill this holy mead with their energy so that all who partake of it will be inspired in word and deed. Visualize the energy and feel the power as it fills the horn. At this point you should pour a sacrifice into the *bowli*.

ᘓ **Passing The Horn.** Carry the horn to each person participating in the Blót. Allow them to make a toast to the God/Goddess in words of their choosing. Another way we do this is to allow everyone to approach the altar one at a time, make a toast and pour a sacrifice into the bowl.

ᘓ **Offer Up Sacrifice.** Hold the bowl up high and offer up the sacrifice, saying: "(God/Goddess), we offer you this sacrifice not of blood, as in days of old, but of our struggles and devotion. May the mingling of our energies strengthen us all—Gods and Man alike."

ᘓ **The Blessing.** Go to each person with the bowl and sprig, and dip the sprig into the mead. Sprinkle each person with a special blessing of the God/Goddess (i.e. "In the name of the mighty Thor, may you find strength as you battle your enemies...").

ᘓ **Closing.** Thank the God/Goddess for their time and energy. and remember the bond you now have with them.

Ritual Tools

ça **Gandr.** The *Gandr* is a wand upon which is engraved the runes of the Elder Futhark. These are mystical symbols representing the various powers of nature and the universe. The *Gandr* represents the staff of Odin.

ça **Antler.** The antler is associated with the God Frey, because of an allusion in the prose Edda to an earlier myth in which Frey goes into battle with Beli armed only with a hart's horn.

ça **Sword.** The sword is a ritual tool used in the Tyr-Blót, as Tyr is associated with war and the martial virtues. Oaths are sworn on swords as in the ancient times, bridging the connection between Tyr and the concepts of justice and order. The sword is also utilized for the Baldr-Blót, because this God symbolizes the noble warrior. Indeed, his name means "bold", and the warrior's death is rebirth. For prison use, the sword is usually made of cardboard and painted; however, wooden swords are available for purchase through the World Tree Publications catalog, if security in your yard permits this.

ça **Thor's Hammer.** Thor's Hammer is a standard tool at all Blóts and gatherings. Most generally, it plays a vital role in the Thor-Blót, standing for the power of defense and protection. A Thor's Hammer amulet is ritually required to be worn by all Kinsmen of our tradition. A large hammer for ritual use should be made from Oak and have the Thurisaz rune carved or drawn on it.

ça **Drinking Horn.** The Drinking Horn holds the mead which represents the sacrifices offered to the deity. In the horn, the mead is the medium infused with the power of the God or Goddess, through which divine energy is transmitted to the participants at a rite. One large ceremonial horn and individual horns for each kindred member are required.

ça **Bowli.** The *bowli* holds a portion of the mead sacrifice from the ceremonial horn. This is a bowl, usually handmade from oak.

Mead remaining in the *bowli* after the Blót should be reverently returned to the earth as an offering of gratitude.

- **Evergreen.** A sprig of evergreen is utilized at every gathering. Evergreen stands for the life force and is used to sprinkle the participants in a ritual with the divinely charged mead. When cutting a sprig, you must ask permission from the tee, explaining your reason for taking it. After the gathering or Blót, return the branch to the base of the tree from which it was cut, so that it will decay and ultimately be reintegrated into the tree.

- **Altar.** The altar is an integral part of all gatherings. The Altar sits on the Northern wall of the longhouse, facing South. The Altar can be made of stone or pole construction and stands as a permanent aspect of sanctified ground and nature.

- **Sunwheel.** The sunwheel, sign of the All-Father, sits on the Altar. This honors not only the All-Father, but nature and the sun.

- **Mead.** Mead is an integral part of all gatherings for honoring the Gods and ancestors. For those in a situation of confinement, mead can be substituted with juice or water.

- **Runes.** Each member should have a personal set of twenty-four Runes for mystery and health. These help tell the story of our belief.

- **Firewood.** Firewood is used for open fire and for meditation in the ritual area.

- **Kindred Banner/Shield.** The kindred banner or shield should be about two feet by three feet and should be designed by the kindred.

- **Ásatrú Flag.** The Ásatrú flag can be purchased from World Tree Publications. Flag contains a spread Raven on white with three runes of mystery emblazed.

Kindred-Recognized Holy Days

Like all religions, Ásatrú requires special preparations of time, place, food, and tools for our rituals. For those incarcerated, there are other items necessary for the education of our kindred, such as a room in the chapel to hold study meetings to review videos and listen to tapes. The ability to purchase rune stones and other religious materials, such as books, Thor's Hammers, tunics, etc., is also helpful.

We have many customs surrounding our seasonal rites. For example, Yule (December 21) is the night before the Winter Solstice, the time when the new year is born. We honor the beginning of the Sun's return and the breaking of Winter's spell. We hail Thor and have a feast of goat, fresh vegetables, fresh bread, fruit, and nuts. We likewise decorate a tree with Sunwheels, and burn a Yule log at the day's end. As another example, on the first of May we celebrate the birth of spring and the coming of Freya. During this day we participate in games, such as the Caber Toss (an 8'6" x 6"pole thrown for distance), the Hammer Throw (a large weight with a rope and T-handle thrown for distance), and the tug of war over a mud pit. The day ends with a blessing by the Goði. We understand that people may not be able to celebrate the Blóts, Feasts, and Sumbels on specific dates due to restraints imposed upon them by correctional facilities, family or work obligations, so we purposely left many dates open (except for Ásatrú High Holy Days which are denoted by an asterisk). We recommend that you celebrate the Holy Days specified on those dates, even if you can only say a simple prayer and meditate upon its meaning. When picking a date to celebrate the Holy Days we left open, we suggest you use one of the numbered days that has a significance in our lore or mythology (i.e. 3, 9, 12, 18).

This calendar is the one that our Kindred follows. Many of the days of remembrance are celebrated by the Ásatrú Alliance, while some are only celebrated by our kindred. For example, our kindred has dedicated the month of May to our Celtic cousins.

Snowmoon / January

Blót: Charming of the Plow *(Date Open)*. In January we plant the seeds for a bountiful harvest. These seeds can be a metaphor for planting the seeds of knowledge or the seeds of strength.

Days of Remembrance

Tyr's Sacrifice *(January 24)*. Today we reflect upon Tyr sacrificing his hand in order to bind Fenris. Reflect upon the sacrifices we made for the benefit of others, or contemplate on an aspect of your character over which you would like beter control, and pray to Tyr for his assistance.

Feast of Þorri *(Date Open)*. Þorri is the Old Norse name for January and also the name of the Icelandic spirit of winter. Pick a day to hold a feast and give honor Þorri and Thor.

Grettir The Strong *(Date Open)*. Grettir was accused of crimes he did not commit, suffered a life of outlawry, and was eventually killed.

Rauðr the Strong *(Date Open)*. Rauðr was a landowner in Norway who was put to death by Olaf Tryggvason for his loyalty to Ásatrú by having a snake forced down his throat. Today, raise a horn to honor him and his kinsmen who gave their lives, rather than convert to Christianity.

Horning / February

Blót: SigrBlót *(Date Open)*. Our kindred celebrates this Blót to Tyr to remember the importance of holding true to your oath, and the penalty you will pay for breaking it. At this Blót, many kindreds will tell the story of Tyr sacrificing his hand to bind the wolf. This shows us the penalty paid for breaking your word, even for Gods.

Days of Remembrance

Eyvind Kinnrifi *(Date Open)*. Olaf Tryggvason tortured him to death by placing a bowl of red-hot embers on his stomach until his body burst open. Eyvind's only crime was his loyalty to the Old Ways.

Barri *(Date Open)*. This is the day we celebrate the wooing by Ingvi Frey of the maiden Gerðr, a symbolic marriage of the Vanir God of Fertility with the Mother Earth. It is a festival of fertility, the planted seed and the plowed furrow. For those of you who garden, this is the time to plant seeds indoors, to later be transplanted in the summer garden.

Feast of Vali *(Date Open)*. This feast originally celebrated the death of Höðr at the hands of Vali. This late winter festival relates to the triumphant return of the light of the sun over the dark days of winter. Today it is a traditional celebration of the family. A time for the customary exchange of cards and gifts with loved ones. It is also a time for the renewal of marriage vows and an occasion for marriages.

Loretta Bailey *(February 24)*. Tyrsoak remembers his Grandmother telling stories of her family coming from Ireland and giving him advice to always keep his word no matter how hard it is. Those two things sparked his interest in the Old Ways and made him the man he is today.

Lenting / March

Blót: *Feast of Ostara *(March 20 or 21)*. Our kindred celebrates the fruition of the seeds planted in January. We look and see Mother Earth coming to life and celebrate the rebirth of nature and the new hopes of their Folk. AsaFolk honor the Mother aspects of Frigg, Freya, and Nerthus.

Days of Remembrance

Birth of Our Kindred *(March 17)*. Our kindred was established on March 17, 2013 to keep the Old Ways alive through education, ritual, and deed.

Feast of Heimdall *(Date Open)*. Hold a feast to honor the vigilent guard of the Bifröst bridge.

Ragnar Loðbrok *(March 28)*. We remember Ragnar, one of the most famous Vikings, who raided Paris on Easter Sunday in the Runic Year 1145. Raise a horn in his honor and read from his Saga.

Oliver the Martyr *(Date Open)*. An adherent of Ásatrú who persisted in organizing underground sacrifices to the Gods and Goddesses despite decrees by Olaf "The Lawbreaker" Tryggvason forbidding such activities. Betrayed by an informer, he was killed by Olaf's men while preparing for the Spring sacrifice in the village of Maerin, Norway.

Ostara / April

Blót: Thor-Blót *(Date Open)*. We ask Thor to protect us and give us strength for the battles ahead. At this Blót everyone should look inward to discover where they need Thor's strength to overcome the negative aspect in their lives which seeks to hold us back or bring us down. We call upon Thor to break down the barriers that hold us back and to give us strength to overcome what we are battling.

Days of Remembrance

Hakon "The Great" Sigurðson *(Date Open)*. Defender of the Old Ways in Norway. Jarl Hakon restored the worship of the Old Gods and cast out the alien religion. Hakon's defense of our ancestral ways helped encourage the survival of our traditions in Iceland, where they eventually became the seeds of modern-day Ásatrú. On this day, reflect on how the actions of the individual can impact world events and the future of Ásatrú.

Sumarsdag *(Date Open)*. Today we celebrate the first day of Summer in the Old Icelandic calendar. In Iceland it had strong agricultural overtones, but elsewhere in the Nordic world, it was a time to sacrifice to Odin for victory in the summer voyages and battles.

Yggdrasill Day *(Date Open)*. On this day we realize the great significance that the World Tree plays in our culture, heritage, and native spirituality. It is from the World Tree that we came, and it shelters and nurtures the Ásatrú today, and will offer refuge to the Folk come Ragnarok. Trees are the lungs as well as the soul of Midgard. Plant a tree today, nurture it, and protect it.

Walburg *(Date Open)*. This is better known as Walpurgisnacht or May Eve. Walberg is a goddess of our folk, combining some of the traits of her better-known peers. Reflect this day on Freya, Hel, and Frigg as the repository of the glorious dead, and you will have an idea of Walburg's nature. On this day, pour a horn of mead upon the earth in memory of our heroes.

Merrymoon / May:

Blót: May Day *(May 1)*. We ask Freya to bless the seeds which are planted with our hopes and aspirations. Many kindreds actually plant flower seeds and give their children seeds to plant as a way of getting them involved and explaining to them the reasons for planting the seeds at that time of year. This is the time many of our kindred take on new members to sow the seeds of knowledge. We also celebrate the kinship with our Celtic cousins.

Days of Remembrance

Guðroðr or **Guðbrandsdal** *(Date Open)*. He had his tongue cut out for organizing a rebellion against Olaf "The Lawbreaker" Tryggvason's violent conversion methods to Christianity.

Suibhne Geilt, "Mad Sweeney" *(Date Open)*. Mad Sweeney was a Celtic Shaman who was touched with divine inspiration. He was able to grow feathers and become a bird. He is an excellent source to call upon to learn about Celtic magic and shaMánism.

Caþbhadh "Battle-Slayer" *(Date Open)*. Caþbhadh was the most a famous Irish Druid that trained many Irish warriors in magical arts. He was so skilled in battle magic that he gained the name "Battle-Slayer". Many legends claim he can affect the future with magic. He is an excellent source to strengthen your magical skills.

Cu Chulainn *(Date Open)*. Cu Chulainn is said to have been born three times to three different fathers. He was a celebrated Red Branch knight and wielded his barbed spear, Gae Bulga. He was a gifted Celtic Berserker and was known as the perfect warrior trained in combat: mental, spiritual and magical.

Fionn mac Cumhaill *(Date Open)*. Fionn was a great war leader who led the Fianna. He accidentally consumed three drops containing magic from the Salmon of Wisdom and thus gained infinite wisdom. He is known as the Champion of the oppressed.

Midyear / June:

Blót: *Midsummer (June 21).* We prepare for the dark days ahead as Sunna begins her decline. We reflect on Baldr's life and how someone in Hel has a chance to come back. The slaying of Baldr should be told and then reflected upon. Some kindreds even act this out as a play to entertain guests and those who do not know the story.

Days of Remembrance

Lindisfarne Day *(June 8).* On this day in the Runic Year 1043 three Viking ships raided the isle of Lindisfarne, officially opening what is known as the Viking Age. Raise a horn to these brave warriors who began the resistance of the alien invasion of the Northlands and sought revenge for the slaughter of the Saxons by Charlemagne.

Ásatrú Alliance Founding Day *(June 19).* On this date in the year 2238 R.E., seven Kindreds of the former Ásatrú Free Assembly joined together by ratifying a set of bylaws to preserve and continue to promote the cause of the AFA and Ásatrú in Vinland. On this day, reflect on what you can do to preserve our folkways.

Sigurð the Volsung *(Date Open).* He is the model Germanic hero. His wooing of the Valkyrie Brynhild, winning the treasure of the Nibelungs, and the constant theme of Odinic initiation that weaves itself throughout his story are priceless parts of our Ásatrú heritage.

Haymoon / July:

Blót: Thing-Blót *(Date Open).* We look to Tyr and reflect upon the importance of the law of the Folk. This is the time to ensure that Folk Law has not strayed from Natural Law. Most kindreds recite some aspect of the Law just as the Lawspeaker would at the Althing in Iceland. The kindred bylaws would be perfect for prison kindreds and freeworld kindreds alike.

Days of Remembrance

Founder's Day *(July 4).* On this day we honor the unselfish personal sacrifice and unswerving dedication to our Folk exemplified by the founders of modern era Ásatrú, H. Rud Mills of Australia,

Sveinbjorn Beinteinsson and Thorsteinn Guthjonson of Iceland. On this day, reflect on what you can do to promote the growth of our ancestral religion and protect our sacred heritage and traditions.

Unn the Deep-Minded *(Date Open)*. Unn was a powerful figure from the Laxdaela Saga who emigrated to Scotland to avoid the hostility of King Harald Finehair. She established dynasties in the Orkney and Faroe Islands by carefully marrying off her grand-daughters. As a settler in Iceland, she continued to exhibit all those traits of her hallmark strong will.

Stikklestad Day *(July 29)*. Olaf "The Lawbreaker" Tryggvason was killed at the Battle of Stikklestad on this date in the Runic Era year 1280. Olaf acquired a reputation for killing, maiming, and exiling his fellow Norweigans who would not convert to Christianity. Today we honor the Ásatrú martyrs who died rather than submitting to his will.

Mindaugas of Lithuania *(Date Open)*. Beginning in 1199, the Roman Catholic Church declared crusades against Baltic pagans. Grand Duke Mindaugas stood against the crusaders and continued to worship pagan deities such as Perkunas, who mirrors our Thor.

Harvest / August:

Blót: Freyfaxi *(Date Open)*. Freyfaxi marked the time of the Harvest Festival when we feast in honor of Frey, God of the Harvest. It is a time of rejoicing and reaping what has been sown. This is the time to sacrifice your very best. In olden times our ancestors held horse races and had a great feast in which the winning horse was sacrificed to Frey.

Days of Remembrance

Radboð *(Date open)*. A King of Frisia who refused conversion so as not to be separated from his ancestors. On this date we honor Radboð a king of Frisia who was an early target Christian missionaries. Just before his baptism ceremony, he asked the clergy what fate his befallen ancestors who died loyal to Ásatrú. The missionaries replied that Radboð's Heathen ancestors were burning in Hell. To which the king replied: "Then I will rather live there with my ancestors than go to heaven with a parcel of beggars." The baptism was cancelled, the aliens expelled, and Frisia remained free. Drink a horn this day in memory of Radboð.

Shedding / September

Blót: *WinterFinding, the Autumnal Equinox *(September 22 or 23)*. We brace ourselves for longer nights and the onset of winter. We call upon Odin for inspiration and wisdom during the Fall Festival and the celebration of the last harvest. We traditionally take inventory of our supplies and determine how we will survive the winter with what we have.

Days of Remembrance

Erik the Victorious *(Date Open)*. A Swedish king who abandoned Christianity for the Old Ways and won the Battle of Fyrisvellir after sacrificing to Odin.

Herman of the Cherusci *(Date Open)*. A leader of the tribe called Cherusci defeated Varus' three Roman Legions in 9 C.E. He blocked our amalgamation into the Mediterranean morass. Herman was very aware of his duties not only as a member of his tribe but also as an Asaman.

Hunting / October

Blót: Winter Nights/VetraBlót *(Date Open)*. In the Old Nordic calendar, winter begins on the Saturday between October 11 and October 17, so pick a date between those two dates for this Blót. Winter nights celebrates the bounty of the harvest and honors the Goddess Freya and the fertility spirits called Disir (often the Disir are seen as our female ancestors). Give glory to Freya and pour a libation of ale, mead, milk, or juice into the soil as an offering to the Disir and the Earth itself.

Days of Rememberance

Erik The Red *(Date Open)*. The founder of Greenland and father of Leif Erikson the founder of Vinland. Erik remained loyal to Thor even when his wife converted to Christianity and refused to sleep with her Heathen husband.

Disir Blót *(Date Open)*. On this date we raise a horn to our deceased relatives and praise their worthy deeds. Some of us do a Blót to Hel and ask her to bring messages or gifts to our ancestors.

Leif Erikson *(Date Open)*. In this month Leif beat Columbus to the shores of Vinland by over five hundred years.

Fogmoon / November

Blót: Feast of Einherjar *(November 11)*. This is the feast of the Heroes of Valhöll. This Blót is held in honor of Odin and we pay our respects to the heroes of the Folk. This is a good Blót to boast of the things you have done which feel make you worthy of a place in Odin's hall.

Days of Remembrance

Heroes of Midgard *(Date Open)*. We celebrate our fallen heroes of Midgard who have sacrificed their lives to bring the Old Ways back to us. Raise a horn today to whoever comes to mind.

Queen Sigriðr of Sweden *(Date Open)*. Defender of the Old Ways in Sweden. Olaf "The Lawbreaker" Tryggvason asked for her hand in marriage and then demanded she convert to Christianity, which she refused. He slapped her face and called the wedding off. This deprived Olaf of political power that he could have used to accelerate the Christianization of Scandinavia. History tells us that the Heathens held on for over 300 more years in the Northlands.

Feast of Ullr *(Date Open)*. The Feast of Ullr is to celebrate the Hunt and gain personal luck needed for success. Weapons are dedicated on this day to Ullr, God of the Bow. In ancient times, if your hunting arms were blessed by the luck of the God of the Hunt, your family and tribe shared the bounty with a Blót and Feast to Ullr.

Yule / December

Blót: *Mother Night *(December 20 or 21)*. As the night before the Winter Solstice, this is the time when the New Year is born. We honor Thor who broke winter's back. It is recommended that everyone does some form of ritual every day until the 31st.

Twelfth Night *(December 31)*. This culminates the traditional twelve days of Yule, each day of which is a month of the preceding year in miniature. Reflect on the past year. Take stock and lay a course for the future. Make New Year's resolutions in the old way by swearing your oath to Frey's boar or on your Hammer.

Days of Remembrance

High Feast of Yule *(December 22)*. Beginning of Runic Year, sacred to Thor and Frey.

Egil Skallagrimsson *(Date Open)*. Odin was his God, and the blood of berserkers and shape-shifters ran in his family. His lust for fame and gold was insatiable. yet the same man was passionately moved by the love of his friends and generously open-handed to those who found his favor.

From his weapons away no one should ever
Stir one step on the field,
For no one knows when need might have
On a sullen man of his sword.
-The Hávámal

Seasonal Rituals

Snowmoon/January: Charming of the Plow

This blót was an agricultural ritual in olden times, as most of our ancestors were farmers. So we honor a God or Goddess of fertility as we plant seeds to bring forth new life, be it a plant or an idea. You will need some bread or cake to use later in the blót.

(NOTE: Some kindreds chose to blót to Odin and Frigg at this time. If you choose to Blót to them, you'll need to modify this Blót accordingly.)

Required Tools

- ᛟ Antler
- ᛟ Mead
- ᛟ Evergreen sprig
- ᛟ Bowli
- ᛟ Horn
- ᛟ Loaf of bread or small cake

Hallowing

Set up the altar in the west, the direction of Vanaheim. While holding an antler in your sword hand, assume the Elhaz stance with your legs together and arms up at a 45-degree angle. If you cannot use a stag or deer antler, a cardboard or wooden replica will suffice. Take a moment to connect with Ingwaz—Frey's energy. When you are ready, face West and trace the Ingwaz rune while vibrating its name. Envision it glowing yellowish-green and say:

"Hjartar í Vestri helga vé þetta ok hindra alla illska."

(Yartar e Vestray hel-gah vay they-ta uck hindra alla ill-ska.)

Turn to the North, trace the Ingwaz rune while vibrating its name, envision the rune glowing yellowish-green, and say:

"Hjartar í Norðri helga vé þetta ok hindra alla illska."

(Yartar e Northray hel-gah vay they-ta uck hindra alla ill-ska.)

Turn to the East, trace the Ingwaz rune while vibrating its name, envision the rune glowing yellowish-green, and say:

"Hjartar í Austri helga vé þetta ok hindra alla illska."

(Yartar e Austray hel-gah vay they-ta uck hindra alla ill-ska.)

Turn to the South, trace the Ingwaz rune while vibrating its name, envision the rune glowing yellowish-green, and say:

"Hjartar í Suðri helga vé þetta ok hindra alla illska."

(Yartar e Soothray hel-gah vay they-ta uck hindra alla ill-ska.)

Return to the west, look up and trace the Ingwaz rune above you while vibrating its name, envision the rune glowing yellowish-green, and say:

"Hjartar í yfir mér helga vé þetta ok hindra alla illska."

(Yartar e oof-er meer hel-gah vay they-ta uck hindra alla ill-ska.)

Look at the ground below, trace the Ingwaz rune while vibrating its name, envision the rune glowing yellowish-green, and say:

"Hjartar í undir mér helga vé þetta ok hindra alla illska."

(Yartar e under meer hel-gah vay they-ta uck hindra alla ill-ska.)

(These translate to: Antler in the West/North/East/South/Over/Under, hallow and hold this sacred stead.)

With arms outstretched, say:

"As Heimdall guards the Bifröst Bridge, may this *vé* be protected from all unholy or unharmonious wights and ways."

Consecrate Altar

Face west again, and using an antler, make the Ingwaz sign over the altar while saying: "I consecrate and make holy this altar. This land and all upon it in the name of Frey. May our hearts and minds be pure for the working here this day as we seek to strengthen Mother Earth and bring forth new life. Hail Frey! Hail Frey! Hail Frey!"

Invite Deity

Begin with a call such as these below:

"Hail Frey, God of fertility, bringer of new life."

"Hail Odin, God of wisdom and exploration."

"Hail Thor, God who brings the rain."

"Hail Freya, Goddess of fertility, beautiful maiden."

"Hail Frigg, Goddess of Mothers, Mother to us all."

"Hail Iðunn, Goddess of youth, guardian of the God's fruits."

"Hail Land-wights, spirits of the Land."

Then say: "We call to you all to join us this day as we gather to honor Mother Earth, and strive to strengthen Her as She has strengthened us. What we plant today brings forth a new life for tomorrow. Hail new life! Hail new life! Hail new life!"

Reading or Explanation

At this point you can read something from the myths or sagas, or recite a poem—anything that will help those gathered understand the importance of why you all have come together at this time. For example, the story of Iðunn and her apples is a good tale to read.

Charge the mead

Traditionally the Goði (priest) will fill the horn with mead, then make the sign of the Ingwaz rune over it three times while vibrating its name, and say:

"We welcome your presence in this holy *vé*, and we offer you sacrifice. We come to you with this gift of our efforts, struggles, and devotion. May this sacrifice aid us, Gods and men alike, against those who would wage war against Asgard or seek to enslave us in mind or body in Midgard."

The Goði then holds up the horn and says:

"We call upon you Frey and the Gods and Goddesses of old to join together this day and pour forth energy into this sacred mead. Strengthen your children here in Midgard as we strive to bring forth a new life, and a new beginning for us all. Accept our gifts, not as slaves, for we have no master. We bow before no Man and yield only to Gods. We offer these gifts not in appeasement, for we stand in good stead with you, but as a sign of our kinship and fellowship."

Lower the horn, look into it and search for the answer you seek or wait until you feel the energy filling the horn.

Sacrifice

Carry the horn of mead around the circle. Allow each person to raise the horn and speak their own words to the Gods and Goddesses. then allow them to pour some into the *bowli*.

Using a loaf of bread or small cake, give everyone a piece to hold then say: "Mother Earth, you have strengthened us all of our life. Your children gather together now to remember you and to offer sacrifice as a family gathering to please their Mother. Accept our sacrifice and smile upon your children once again."

The group offers the bread or cake at the same time, saying: "Thank you, Mother Earth, for all you do."

The Blessing

Using the remaining bread or cake, the Goði or person leading the blót will give each person a piece while saying something special to them, such as: "Eat and gain strength from Mother Earth!" "May this blessing bring forth new life or new ideas!" "Be thankful for the blessings from Mother Earth!"

Closing

Stand in the direction to the west at the altar and say: "We thank the Gods and Goddesses of the folk, the mighty Frey and beautiful Freya, and the spirits of the land. May the work done here today strengthen us all. Fare well on your journey homeward."

Take up the antler and face west. Make the sign of Ingwaz and vibrate its name.

Turn to the north, make the sign of Ingwaz and vibrate its name.

Turn to the east, make the sign of Ingwaz and vibrate its name.

Turn to the south, make the sign of Ingwaz and vibrate its name. When you return to the west, say: "This blót is now ended."

Ðorning/February: Sigrblót

This blót to Tyr reminds us of the consequences of making an oath and holding true to your word, or paying the penalty for breaking it. Tyr is a great example of someone stepping forward to do what needs to be done, regardless of the cost.

Required Tools

- ℞ Sword.
- ℞ Mead.
- ℞ Evergreen sprig.
- ℞ Bowli.
- ℞ Horn.

Have the altar set up beforehand with the ritual tools on it. If you have a larger group, you can have some of them participate by carrying the tools and placing them on the altar. I like to walk three times in a circle around the area clockwise, and on the third time place the tools on the altar.

Hallowing

Start in the North, facing the altar with sword in hand, standing in the Elhaz stance, and trace the Teiwaz rune, envision it glowing white, and call out:

"Sverd í Norðri helga vé þetta ok hindra alla illska."

Turn to the East, draw the Teiwaz rune while vibrating its name, envision it glowing white, and say:

"Sverd í Austri helga vé þetta ok hindra alla illska."

Turn to the South, draw the Teiwaz rune while vibrating its name, envision it glowing white, and say:

"Sverd í Suðri helga vé þetta ok hindra alla illska."

Turn to the West, draw the Teiwaz rune while vibrating its name, envision it glowing white, and say:

"Sverd í Vestri helga vé þetta ok hindra alla illska."

Return to the North, look up, draw the Teiwaz rune while vibrating its name, envision it glowing white, and say:

"Sverd í yfir mér helga vé þetta ok hindra alla illska."

Look down, draw the Teiwaz rune while vibrating its name, envision it glowing white, and say:

"Sverd í undir mér helga vé þetta ok hindra alla illska."

With arms outstretched, say:

"As Heimdall guards the Bifröst Bridge, may this vé be protected from all unholy or unharmonious wights and ways."

Consecrate Altar

Still holding the sword, carve a Teiwaz rune in the air over the altar, saying:

"I consecrate and make holy this altar, this land and all upon it in the name of Tyr. May our hearts and minds be pure for the workings here this day. Hail Tyr, Hail Tyr, Hail Tyr."

Calling

Standing at the altar with sword raised in the Elhaz stance, call out the following:

"Tyr, Tyr, Tyr, ancient Sky Father of Old. God of sacrifice, God of justice, God of right action. Join us here this day as we remember the importance of making an oath. It is the story of your sacrifice which teaches us the true meaning of an oath, for both good and ill."

Reading or Explanation

I like to read the story of Tyr sacrificing his hand to bind the wolf. You can also explain how an oath affects your *orlog* and *Wyrd*, how it binds those around you to the cause and effect of you keeping it, and the penalties involved in breaking it. This helps everyone get focused on the importance of the blót and taking an oath.

Charge the mead

Traditionally the Goði (priest) will fill the horn with mead, then make the sign of the Teiwaz rune three times, and while vibrating its name, say: "We welcome your presence in this holy vé, and we offer you sacrifice. We come to you with this gift of our efforts, struggles, and devotion. May this sacrifice aid us, Gods and men alike, against those who would wage war against Asgard or seek to enslave us in mind or body in Midgard."

The Goði then holds up the horn and says:

"Tyr – Tyr – Tyr ancient Sky Father. It is your rune our ancestors carved on their weapons for victory to give them strength in battle. We call upon you today to fill this horn with your energy, to give us strength to uphold the oaths we swear, and to strive forward doing what is right and noble. Accept our gifts, not as slaves, for we have no master. We bow before no man and yield only to Gods. We offer these gifts not in appeasement, for we stand in good stead with you; but as a sign of our kinship and fellowship."

Lower the horn, visualize the energy and feel the power as it fills the horn. Pour some of the charged mead into the bowli.

Sacrifice

Allow everyone to approach the altar, raise a horn to Tyr, speak aloud if they wish, and then pour a sacrifice into the bowli. (Some kindreds allow members to take an oath at this time, but everyone present should be in agreement beforehand as it is a very serious matter.) Then hold the bowli up and say:

"Tyr, we offer you this sacrifice, not of blood as in days of old, but of our devotion and struggles. May the mingling of our energies strength us all, Gods and Man alike. Hail, hail, hail!"

The Blessing

Dip the evergreen sprig into the bowli and sprinkle each celebrant, saying: "May Tyr, the Lord of Swords, grant you strength and victory."

Walk up to each person, clasp their right arm on the bicep and say:

"Tyr sacrificed his right arm to protect the Gods, and may you be willing to sacrifice what is needed to protect the Gods and Man. May Tyr's strength be seen in your actions."

Closing

"Tyr, we thank you for all you have given us and as we go forth may our actions make you proud. May your example be seen in our lives. Fare well on your journey homeward."

Take up the sword and face North. Make the sign of Teiwaz and vibrates its name.

Turn to the East, make the sign of Teiwaz, and vibrate its name.

Turn to the South, make the sign of Teiwaz, and vibrate its name.

Turn to the West, make the sign of Teiwaz, and vibrate its name.

Returning to the North, say: "This blót is now ended!"

Lenting/March 20:
Spring Equinox and Feast of Ostara

On March 20 we celebrate the rebirth of nature and the beginning of new life. Have the altar set up beforehand with the ritual tools on it. If you have a larger group, you can have some of them participate by carrying the tools and placing them on the altar. I like to walk three times in a circle around the area clockwise, and on the third time place the tools on the altar.

Required Tools

- ≪ Gandr
- ≪ Mead
- ≪ Evergreen sprig
- ≪ Bowli
- ≪ Horn

Hallowing

Start in the North, facing the altar, with gandr in hand. Standing in the Elhaz stance, trace the Berkano rune while vibrating its name. Envision it glowing pale blue, and say:

"Gandr í Norðri helga vé þetta ok hindra alla illska."

Turn to the East, trace the Berkano rune while vibrating its name, envision it glowing pale blue, and say:

"Gandr í Austri helga vé þetta ok hindra alla illska."

Turn to the South, trace the Berkano rune while vibrating its name, envision it glowing pale blue, and say:

"Gandr í Suðri helga vé þetta ok hindra alla illska."

Turn to the West, trace the Berkano rune while vibrating its name, envision it glowing pale blue, and say:

"Gandr í Vestri helga vé þetta ok hindra alla illska."

Return to the North, look up, trace the Berkano rune while vibrating its name, envision it glowing pale blue, and say:

"Gandr í yfir mér helga vé þetta ok hindra alla illska."

Look down, trace the Berkano rune while vibrating its name, envision it glowing pale blue, and say:

"Gandr í undir mér helga vé þetta ok hindra alla illska."

With arms outstretched, say: "As Heimdall guards the Bifröst Bridge, may this vé be protected from all unholy or unharmonious wights and ways."

Consecrate Altar

Make the sign of the Berkano rune over the altar and say:

"I consecrate this altar and all upon it in the name of Frigg, Nerthus, and Ostara. I consecrate this holy space and all who stand upon it in their names. May our hearts and mind be pure for the workings here this day, while we honor Mother Earth."

Calling

While standing in the Elhaz stance with arms raised upward, repeat the following:

"Hail to you. Mother; you are known by many names. and we call out to you this day..." Then have each person call out one of Mother Earth's names: i.e. Hail Frigg, Nerthus, Jord, Ostara. etc.)

"We ask you to join your children in Midgard as we sacrifice our very best to strengthen you as you have strengthened us throughout our life. Hold us this day in your bosom once again and let us feel the love that only a Mother can give. Remind us all this day of the importance of a loving family and new life as we see the world come to life around us once again."

Address the Kindred or Tell Story

At this point you can address the kindred, reminding them why we are all here and the importance of this day, or tell a story which deals with new birth or life. You could say:

"This day symbolizes the rebirth of all this around us, we see Mother Earth come to life around us. See the beauty of our mother. Think of our children as they grow. Think of how our mother nourishes us. Hail to our Mother! Hail to our Mother! Hail to our Mother!"

Charging the mead

Traditionally the Goði (priest) will fill the horn with mead, then make the sign of the Berkano rune over it three times, and while vibrating its name, say: "We welcome your presence in this holy vé, and we offer you sacrifice. We come to you with this gift of our efforts, struggles, and devotion. May this sacrifice aid us, Gods and men alike, against those who would wage war against Asgard or seek to enslave us in mind or body in Midgard."

The Goði then holds up the horn and says: "Mother, it is you who nurtures your children. Through your gifts we, your children, grow and become strong. We ask for your blessing and energy to fill this holy drink with your power so that we, your children, can drink and become even stronger in the days ahead. Accept our gifts, not as slaves, for we have no master. We bow before no man and Yield only to Gods. We offer these gifts not in appeasement, for we stand in good stead with you; but as a sign of our kinship and fellowship."

Lower the horn to your waist. Look into it and search and feel for the energy that your Mother will provide. Then pour a small amount into the bowli.

Sacrifice

At this point you can have each person approach the altar, raise the horn, speak words aloud or to themselves, and then pour a bit of the horn into the bowli or directly on Mother Earth. Alternately you can carry the horn around to each person and let them raise the horn and speak, then pour a sacrifice onto Mother Earth.

Blessing

Raise the bowli above your head and say: "Mother, may our combined sacrifices strengthen you as you have strengthened us. May we each receive your special blessing this day. Hail."

Carry the bowli and a sprig, walk up to each person, and using the sprig and mead in the bowli, sprinkle them with a special blessing for each person. For example: "May our Mother strengthen you in the way you seek." "May our Mother's blessing make you fertile." "May our Mother's gifts open your eyes to a new life." "May our Mother's love make you feel a part of our family."

Sacrifice Combined Energy in Bowli

Standing in the North, hold the bowli in front of you and say,

"Mother, we thank you for your gifts, and for the blessings we have received this day. We offer you our sacrifices this day as our gift to strengthen you in your time of need. May we all go forth together with a newfound strength and desire to love and care for our families and for you, Mother Earth. Hail Mother Earth! Hail Mother Earth! Hail Mother Earth!"

Pour the contents of the bowli onto a bush, flowers, or the ground.

Closing

While standing in the North, repeat the following: "Mother, this blót is done. yet now our family will Feast and Hold a Holy sumbel. We will hold you in our hearts and mind always. You are with us wherever we go. May our words and deeds make you proud."

Take up the gandr and face North. Make the sign of Berkano and vibrate its name.

Turn to the East, make the sign of Berkano, and vibrate its name.

Turn to the South, make the sign Berkano, and vibrate its name.

Turn to the West, make the sign of Berkano, and vibrate its name.

When you return to the North, say: "This blót is now ended."

It is now time to move onto the Feast and Sumble.

Lenting/March 17: Birth of Our Kindred

On the 17th of Lenting/March we celebrate the anniversary of the birth of our kindred. We hold a blót to honor Odin, Thor and Tyr. Following this blót we have a sumble and a feast followed by nine days of fasting. We fast to connect with Odin as he hung on Yggdrasill.

(Note: We do not advocate fasting if you are on medication or have a medical condition such as diabetes or heart problems. These conditions can cause sometimes fatal complications while fasting.)

Have the ritual tools setup beforehand if this is a solitary blót. If you have a larger group, you can have some of them participate by carrying the tools and placing them on the altar. I like to walk three times in a circle around the area clockwise, and on the third time place the tools on the altar.

Required Tools

- A gandr
- A wooden Thor's hammer
- A sword
- A sunwheel
- A bowli
- A drinking horn
- Mead or juice
- An evergreen sprig
- A set of runes. If this is a solitary blót, use your own set; otherwise you will need to use a group or kindred set.
- An object to scrape the rune with.

Hallowing

Start in the North facing the altar. Stand in the Elhaz stance, raise the Gandr and trace the Ansuz rune while vibrating its name, envision it glowing blue, and say:

"Gandr í Norðri helga vé þetta ok hindra alla illska."

Turn to the East, trace the Ansuz rune while vibrating its name, envision it glowing blue, and say:

"Gandr í Austri helga vé þetta ok hindra alla illska."

Turn to the South, trace the Ansuz rune while vibrating its name, envision it glowing blue, and say:

ODIN'S CHOSEN

111

"Gandr í Suðri helga vé þetta ok hindra alla illska."

Turn to the West, trace the Ansuz rune while vibrating its name, envision it glowing blue, and say:
"Gandr í Vestri helga vé þetta ok hindra alla illska."

Return to the North, look up trace the Ansuz rune while vibrating its name, envision it glowing blue and say:
"Gandr í yfir mér helga vé þetta ok hindra alla illska."

Look down, trace the Ansuz while vibrating its name, envision it glowing blue, and say:
"Gandr í undir mér helga vé þetta ok hindra alla illska."

Place the Gandr on the altar and take up the sword. Trace the Teiwaz rune while vibrating its name, envision it glowing white, and say:
"Sverd í Norðri helga vé þetta ok hindra alla illska."

Turn to the East, trace the Teiwaz rune while vibrating its name, envision it glowing white, and say:
"Sverd í Austri helga vé þetta ok hindra alla illska."

Turn to the South, trace the Teiwaz rune while vibrating its name, envision it glowing white, and say:
"Sverd í Suðri helga vé þetta ok hindra alla illska."

Turn to the West, trace the Teiwaz rune while vibrating its name, envision it glowing white, and say:
"Sverd í Vestri helga vé þetta ok hindra alla illska."

Return to the North, look up, trace the Teiwaz rune while vibrating its name, envision it glowing white, and say:
"Sverd í yfir mér helga vé þetta ok hindra alla illska."

Look down, trace the Teiwaz rune while vibrating its name, envision it glowing white, and say:

"Sverd í undir mér vé þetta ok hindra alla illska."

Place the sword on the altar and pick up the hammer. Face North. trace the Thurisaz rune while vibrating its name, envision it glowing red, and say:

"Hamar í Norðri helga vé þetta ok hindra alla illska."

Turn to the East, trace the Thurisaz rune while vibrating its name, envision it glowing red, and say:

"Hamar í Austri helga vé þetta ok hindra alla illska."

Turn to the South, trace the Thurisaz rune while vibrating its name, envision it glowing red, and say:

"Hamar í Suðri helga vé þetta ok hindra alla illska."

Turn to the West, trace the Thurisaz rune while vibrating its name, envision it glowing red, and say:

"Hamar í Vestri helga vé þetta ok hindra alla illska."

Return to the North, look up, trace the Thurisaz rune while vibrating its name, envision it glowing red, and say:

"Hamar í yfir mér helga vé þetta ok hindra alla illska."

Look down, trace the Thurisaz rune while vibrating its name, envision it glowing red, and say:

"Hamar í undir mér helga vé þetta ok hindra alla illska."

With arms outstretched, say:

"As Heimdall guards the Bifröst Bridge, may this *vé* **be protected from all unholy or unharmonious wights and ways."**

Consecrate the Altar

Using the Gandr, trace the Ansuz rune over the altar and say:

"I hallow this altar, this land and all those upon it in the name of Odin, the All-Father, Ordeal Master, and warrior of warriors."

Take up the sword, trace the Teiwaz rune over the altar and say:

"And I hallow this altar, this land and all those upon it in the name of Tyr, Lord of swords, God of right action, justice, and sacrifice."

Take up the Thor's hammer, trace the Thurisaz rune over the altar and say:

"I also hallow this altar, this land and all those upon it in the name of Thor, protector of Midgard, breaker of barriers, Wielder of Mjölnir. Hail Odin! Hail Tyr! Hail Thor!"

Invocation

"Gods of Asgard: Odin, Tyr, and Thor. We ask you to join us here in Midgard as we offer you sacrifice this day. We ask for your inspiration, guidance and strength throughout this next year, and we offer you thanks for the gifts you have bestowed upon us. Hail Odin! Hail Tyr! Hail Thor!"

Address the Gathered Folk

"We gather here today on the anniversary of the birth of our kindred to celebrate and give thanks. We ask Odin, Tyr, and Thor to teach us, inspire us, guide us, and protect us as we strive to honor them in word and deed and keep the Old Ways alive."

Reflect for a moment or two on the aspects of Odin, Tyr, and Thor that you seek to embody.

Charge the Mead

Fill the horn with mead/juice, then take the sunwheel and hold it above the horn and say:

"Odin, bless this mead and infuse it with your inspiration and wisdom."

Take the Ansuz rune from the set and gently scrape it over the horn so that its shavings fall into the horn. Then make the sign of the Ansuz rune three times over the horn while vibrating its name. Put the rune back on the altar.

Next, take the sword up and hold it above the horn and say: "Tyr, bless this mead and infuse it with your guidance so that we may make the right decisions in our lives."

Take the Teiwaz rune and scrape it over the horn so that its shavings fall into the horn. Then make the sign of the Teiwaz rune three times over the horn while vibrating its name. Put the rune back on the altar.

Finally, take up the Thor's hammer and hold it above the horn and say: "Thor, bless this mead and infuse it with your strength so that we may break any barriers that arise in our lives."

Take the Thurisaz rune and gently scrape it over the horn so that its shavings fall into the horn. Then make the sign of the Thurisaz rune three times over the horn while vibrating its name. Put the rune back on the altar. Then say:

"We welcome your presence in this Holy vé and offer you sacrifice. We come to you with this gift of our efforts, struggles, and devotion. May this sacrifice aid us, Gods and Men alike against those who would wage war against Asgard or seek to enslave us in mind or body in Midgard."

Raise the horn and say:

"Accept our gifts, not as slaves, for we have no master. We bow before no man and yield only to Gods. We offer these gifts not in appeasement, for we stand in good stead with you; but as a sign of our kinship and fellowship."

Lower the horn in front of you until you feel the powers of Odin, Tyr, and Thor flowing into it. Then pour some mead into the bowli as a sacrifice.

Sacrifice

Invite each person one by one to approach the altar. Offer them the horn and say: "May this mead fortify you with the inspiration and wisdom of the All-Father, the guidance of the Lord of Swords, and the strength of Redbeard, the wielder of Mjölnir."

Give each person a chance to raise the horn and address the Gods. They can each take a sip of the holy mead to gain its gifts, and then pour a small portion into the bowli.

Blessing

When everyone has poured their sacrifice into the bowli, hold it in front of you and say: "May our combined sacrifices strengthen both the Gods and Man alike, May the power of Gebo strengthen us all."

Take the sprig and bowli and walk around to each person. Dip the sprig and bless each person saying:

"May the gifts of Odin, Tyr, and Thor fortify you in the days ahead."

After everyone has received a blessing, return to the altar. Hold the bowli above your head and say:

"May the combined energies of the Gods and Man strengthen us all in our time of need. We all strive to keep the Old Ways alive, and we sacrifice our very best to honor you. Hail!"

Pour the bowli onto Mother Earth or into the fire saying:

"This day the Gods have blessed us, in turn we offer up our sacrifices to Mother Earth to strengthen you as it is you who strengthen us all, Gods and Man alike. Hail!"

Closing

Stand in front of the altar and say:

"Odin, All-Father, Harr, we thank you for your gifts. Tyr, Lord of Swords, God of justice and right action, we thank you for your gifts. Thor, Redbeard, protector of Midgard, we thank you for your gifts. We wish you well as you travel homeward. Hail Odin! Hail Tyr! Hail Thor!"

Take up the Gandr and face North. Trace the Ansuz, Teiwaz, and Thurisaz runes while vibrating their names.

Turn to the East, trace the Ansuz, Teiwaz, and Thurisaz runes while vibrating their names.

Turn to the South, trace the Ansuz, Teiwaz, and Thurisaz runes while vibrating their names.

Turn to the West, trace the Ansuz, Teiwaz, and Thurisaz runes while vibrating their names.

Return to the north and say: "This blót is now ended!"

fast To Celebrate The Birth Of Our Kindred

(Note: Do not attempt this fast if you are on medication or have any health problems. If at any time during this fast you become ill, stop immediately and seek medical attention.)

Each year, beginning on the 17th day of March/Lenting, we begin our nine-day fast to celebrate the birth of our kindred. We use this fast to not only celebrate but to purge our body of toxins, strengthen ourselves spiritually, and to share in Odin's suffering when he hung on Yggdrasill for nine days without food or water.

During this fast, we withdraw from the profane to focus on the runes, and the eddas and sagas of our ancestors. We also ask the runes to sustain us on our journey of enlightenment. We have presented this as an incremental fast because a complete fast would cause too much stress on a beginner. Make no mistake, this nine-day incremental fast is a massive undertaking and should not be taken lightly. It will sap you of your strength and test your will, but in the end you will gain a deeper understanding in the runes and you will strengthen the bond between you and Odin. You will need no tools other than your runes. (If you are celebrating the Feast of Ostara, you can postpone the fast or fast through it.)

Daily Ritual

1. Begin the day by reciting our kindred oath, followed by Sigrdrífa's prayer.

2. Hallow your area.

3. Face North, trace the Ansuz rune and say:

"Odin, you hung upon Yggdrasill wounded by your own spear. You sacrificed yourself to yourself. For nine days and nights you suffered without food or water in order to earn the runes. Today I fast in your honor. Hail Odin, Hail Odin, Hail Odin!"

4. Take up your runes, close your eyes and say: "Odin, show me the rune I need to work with today."

5. With your eyes still closed, reach into your rune bag and take up one rune. You may also cast the runes on your altar or altar cloth and blindly take one up.

6. Face North, and trace the rune three times while vibrating its name. Close your eyes and envision it in blazing red.

7. Inhale for a count of three seconds and feel the rune enter with your breath. Hold your breath for a count of three seconds and feel the rune flow through you. Exhale your breath for a count of three seconds, feel the absence of the rune.

8. Repeat this three-count breathing exercise until you feel attuned to the rune.

9. Once you are centered with the rune, say: "(Rune name), give me strength today to continue my fast."

10. You must keep your mind in a spiritual state by avoiding anything that will distract you from connecting with Odin and the rune of the day. Do not watch TV; instead read from the Poetic Edda and any saga of your choice.

11. Before you eat your meal(s), make the sign of the rune over it. Envision the rune fortifying the food. When you eat, feel the rune strengthening your mind, body, and spirit.

Sample Diet

ೞ **Days 1, 2, and 3:** Plan out your meals so that you have a good energy source (fruit, grains, or nuts) and an ample amount of vegetables. You will be only eating two meals on these days. Before you eat, set a portion aside for Odin. Each day, set a larger portion aside for him. Begin to reduce your water intake as well. You want to drink approximately half of what you normally drink.

ର Days 4, 5, and 6: You will be eating a single meal per day. Just as you did in days 1-3, you will set aside a portion for Odin. Reduce your water intake to 1/3 of what you normally drink.

ର Day 7: You will only be drinking 16-20 oz. of juice throughout the day. Offer up a portion to Odin. Limit your water intake to what you feel is appropriate.

ର Day 8: You will only be drinking 8-10 oz. of juice throughout the day. Offer up a portion to Odin. Limit your water intake to what you feel is appropriate.

ର Day 9: No food and only small sips of water throughout the day.

This is merely a dietary suggestion of what has worked for our members. You may remove items as you see fit. For an advanced fast, you can try this:

ର Days 1-3: ½ cup of oatmeal and 1 egg

ର Days 4-6: 8oz. of juice to sip from

ର Days 7-9: Sip water throughout the day

(Note: Keep a candy bar on hand in case you feel faint. Also, it is a good idea to keep a journal of any dreams or visions while on this fast.)

Good luck, and may Odin be with you!

April/Ostara: Blót to Thor

We hold this blót to ask Thor to protect us and give us strength for the battle ahead. At this blót we look inward to discover where we need Thor's strength to overcome the negative aspects in our lives. We ask him to break the barriers that hold us back.

Have the altar set up beforehand with the ritual tools on it. If you have a larger group, you can have some of them participate by carrying the tools and placing them on the altar. I like to walk three times in a circle around the area clockwise, and on the third time place the tools on the altar.

Recommended Tools

- ࠖ A large oak Thor's hammer
- ࠖ A bowli
- ࠖ A horn
- ࠖ Mead
- ࠖ An evergreen sprig

Have the mead or juice to be used open and ready to pour into the horn when needed. It is always best to have someone near you to pour the mead/juice when needed to into the horn.

Before we begin the walk onto sacred land, I always like to take a few minutes to explain what the blót is being held for (i.e. strength, victory, wisdom, etc.). This gives everyone the opportunity to think about which aspect of Thor's strength etc. they need for their own life, and when their turn comes to raise the horn or offer sacrifice they are better prepared for what they want to say or do.

Hallowing

Start in the North, facing the altar. Holding a Thor's hammer in your sword hand, assume the Elhaz stance with your legs together and your arms up in a 45-degree angle. If for whatever reason you cannot use an oak hammer, you can either substitute it with a cardboard replica, or you can make the sign of the Thurisaz rune by making a fist and pushing your thumb between your second and third finger. Take a moment to connect with Thor's protective energy. When you are ready, trace the Thurisaz rune while vibrating its name. Envision it glowing red, and say:

"Hamar í Norðri helga vé þetta ok hindra alla illska."

Turn to the East, trace the Thurisaz rune while vibrating its name, envision the rune glowing red, and say:

"Hamar í Austri helga vé þetta ok hindra alla illska."

Turn to the South, trace the Thurisaz rune while vibrating its name, envision the rune glowing red, and say:
"**Hamar í Suðri helga vé þetta ok hindra alla illska.**"

Turn to the West, trace the Thurisaz rune while vibrating its name, envision the rune glowing red, and say:
"**Hamar í Vestri helga vé þetta ok hindra alla illska.**"

Return to the North, look up, trace the Thurisaz rune while vibrating its name, envision the rune glowing red, and say:
"**Hamar í yfir mér helga vé þetta ok hindra alla illska.**"

Look down, trace the Thurisaz rune while vibrating its name, envision the rune glowing red, and say:
"**Hamar í undir mér Helga vé þetta ok hindra alla illska.**"

With arms outstretched, say:
"As Heimdall guards the Bifröst Bridge, may this *vé* be protected from all unholy or unharmonious wights and ways."

Consecrate Altar

As you return to the North, stand in front of the altar. Using Thor's hammer, make the hammer sign over the altar and say:
"I hallow this altar, this land and those upon it in the name of Thor. May our hearts and minds be pure for the workings here this day. Hail Thor! Hail Thor! Hail Thor!"

Invocation (Inviting Thor)

"Thor, red-bearded brother, protector of the Gods and Man, we ask you to join us here in Midgard as we offer you sacrifice this day. Come and strengthen us in our time of need as we strive to do the work of the Gods here in Midgard. Hail Thor! Hail Thor! Hail Thor!"

Address the Gathered Folk

This is where you remind everyone why you are doing this blót and then take a moment to reflect upon what was said.

"We gather this day as in days of old to honor Thor, Weilder of Mjölnir, protector of the Gods. We are asking for his gifts of strength and protection to help us in our time as we strive to honor the old Gods. Look inward to discover that which you seek, and what you are willing to sacrifice to gain it."

Reflect for a moment or two.

Charge the mead

Traditionally the Goði (priest) will fill the horn with mead, then make the sign of the Thurisaz rune over it three times while vibrating its name, and say:

"We welcome your presence in this holy *vé*, and we offer you sacrifice. We come to you with this gift of our efforts, struggles, and devotion. May this sacrifice aid us, Gods and men alike, against those who would wage war against Asgard or seek to enslave us in mind or body in Midgard."

Standing in front of the altar, raise the horn above your head and say:

"Mighty Thor, protector of the Gods and Man alike. We, your brothers/sisters, here in Midgard call on you this day to give us your strength and protection as we strive to walk the noble path of our ancestors. Fill this sacred mead with your energy so that when it passes our lips your power will flow through our bodies giving us that which we seek. In turn we will sacrifice to you. Accept our gifts, not as slaves, for we have no master. We bow before no man and yield only to Gods. We offer these gifts not in appeasement, for we stand in good stead with you; but as a sign of our kinship and fellowship. Hail Thor! Hail Thor! Hail Thor!"

Lower the horn in front of you until you see or feel the power of Thor flowing into the horn. Pour some of the mead into the bowli as a sacrifice.

Sacrifice

Invite each person one by one to approach the altar or carry the horn around the circle going to each person one by one saying,

"May this holy mead bring you the strength of Thor! May you find that which you seek."

Give each person a chance to raise the horn and say something to Thor in their own words. They can each take a sip of the holy mead to gain a gift, and then either pour a small portion into the bowli or onto the ground. Then hand the horn back to the one passing around the horn.

Blessing

Pour some of the charged mead into the bowli. Hold the bowli in front of you and say:

"May our combined sacrifices strengthen both the Gods and Man alike. Let the power of Gebo strengthen us all."

Take the sprig and bowli and walk around to each person. Dip the sprig into the bowli and mead and bless each person with a different blessing you feel fits them. For example,

"May Thor give you his strength in your time of need; may your actions bring honor to Thor and the folk; may Thor always protect you."

After everyone has received a blessing, return to the altar. Hold the bowli above your head and say:

"May the combined energies of the Gods and Man strengthen us all in our time of need. We all strive to keep the old ways alive. We sacrifice our very best to honor the old one. Hail!"

Pour the mead onto Mother Earth or into the fire saying:

"This day, Thor has blessed us with his strength and protection. In turn the proud men and women here in Midgard offer up our sacrifice to you, Mother Earth, to strengthen you, as it is you who strengthens us all, Gods and Man alike. Hail."

Closing

Stand in front of the altar and say:

"Mighty Thor, red-bearded brother, we thank you for your gifts and we will use them to strengthen us all. We wish you well as you head homeward. Hail Thor! Hail Thor! Hail Thor!"

Take up the hammer and face North. Make the sign of Thurisaz and vibrate its name.

Turn to the East, make the sign of Thurisaz and vibrate its name.

Turn to the South, make the sign of Thurisaz and vibrate its name.

Turn to the West, make the sign of Thurisaz and vibrate its name.

When you return to the North, say:

"This blót is now ended."

Merrymoon/May 1: May Day

This blót is held to signify new life, enjoying the gifts of Mother Earth, and it is held to honor Freya. It is good for strengthing family ties and relationships. and also to strengthen yourself inside with the gifts Mother Earth has given us.

Required Tools

- ❧ Gandr
- ❧ Mead
- ❧ Sunwheel
- ❧ Horn

Have the altar set up beforehand with the ritual tools on it. If you have a larger group, you can have some of them participate by carrying the tools and placing them on the altar. I like to walk three times in a circle around the area clockwise, and on the third time place the tools on the altar.

Hallowing

Set up the altar in the west, the direction of Vanaheim. Assume the Elhaz stance and take a moment to connect with Freya and the Fehu rune. When you are ready, face west with the Gandr in hand. Trace the Fehu rune while vibrating its name, envision it glowing green, and say:

"Gandr í Vestri helga vé þetta ok hindra alla illska."

Turn to the North, trace the Fehu rune while vibrating its name, envision it glowing green, and say:

"Gandr í Norðri helga vé þetta ok hindra alla illska."

Turn to the East, trace the Fehu rune while vibrating its name, envision it glowing green, and say:

"Gandr í Austri helga vé þetta ok hindra alla illska."

Turn to the South, trace the Fehu rune while vibrating its name, envision it glowing green, and say:

"Gandr í Suðri helga vé þetta ok hindra alla illska."

Return to the West, look up, trace the Fehu rune while vibrating its name, envision it glowing green, and say:

"Gandr í yfir mér helga vé þetta ok hindra alla illska."

Look down, trace the Fehu rune while vibrating its name, envision it glowing green, and say:

"Gandr í undir mér helga vé þetta ok hindra alla illska."

With arms outstretched, say:

"As Heimdall guards the Bifröst Bridge, may this *vé* be protected from all unholy or unharmonious wights and ways."

Consecrate Altar

Stand in front of the altar and say:

"I consecrate this altar, this land and all upon it in the name of Freya. May all of us be pure of mind and heart for the workings here this day."

Calling

"Freya, we call upon you this day to join us here in Midgard as we strive to better ourselves and honor our Ancestors. May your blessings this day bring us a new way of looking at life and all it has to offer. Hail Freya! Hail Freya! Hail Freya!"

Reading/Explanation

Tell everyone gathered the purpose for the blót, and what you want them to focus on: i.e. new life, strength, insight, etc. You might also tell a story about Freya.

Charge the mead

Traditionally the Goði (priest) will fill the horn with mead then make the sign of the Fehu rune over it three times. While vibrating its name, say:

"We welcome your presence in this holy vé, and we offer you sacrifice. We come to you with this gift of our efforts, struggles, and devotion. May this sacrifice aid us, Gods and men alike, against those who would wage war against Asgard or seek to enslave us in mind or body in Midgard. Freya, pour forth your energy into this horn so that as it touches our lips, it opens our eyes up to all that surrounds us. May we see the importance of those in our lives, both family and friend. Hail Freya! Hail Freya! Hail Freya!"

The Goði then holds up the horn and says:

"Accept our gifts, not as slaves, for we have no master. We bow to no man and yield only to Gods. We offer these gifts not in appeasement, for we stand in good stead with you; but as a sign of our kinship and fellowship."

Sacrifice

Allow everyone to approach the altar and offer sacrifice to Freya while speaking in their own words, then pour a bit of the mead into the bowli or onto Mother Earth.

Blessing

Using the bowli and a sprig, walk to each person in the circle and sprinkle them with the mead while you give them a personal blessing. For example, "May Freya bring you peace!" "May Freya strengthen you!" "May Freya make you fertile!"

Offer up the bowli; hold it high above your head and say: "Freya, we offer you these gifts out of love. May our sacrifice show our commitment to you and this way of life."

Closing

"Freya, we thank you for your gifts and we hope you will fare us well on our journeys homeward. May you watch proudly as we go forward using your gifts to strengthen the Gods and Man alike. Hail Freya! Hail Freya! Hail Freya!"

Take up the Gandr and face West. Make the sign of Fehu and vibrate its name.

Turn to the North, make the sign of Fehu and vibrate its name.

Turn to the East, make the sign of Fehu and vibrate its name.

Turn to the South, make the sign of Fehu and vibrate its name.

When you return to the West, say: "This blót is now ended."

Midyear/June 21: Midsummer (Summer Solstice)

This Blót is held to Baldr, who was the most beloved of all the Gods. It signifies preparing for the dark days ahead. For those of us in prison, it could also represent our being in prison, away from all those who love us. Just as Baldr resides in Hel until Ragnarök, we are also held here in prison until our day comes and a new beginning is given to us. It is a time to reflect on how to be prepared when the dark days come. What can we do to fight off that which seeks to destroy us or hold us back. The way we conduct ourselves in those times of trouble show our true character.

Required Tools

- ࣸ Gandr
- ࣸ Mead
- ࣸ Sunwheel
- ࣸ Horn

Have the altar set up beforehand with the ritual tools on it. If you have a larger group, you can have some of them participate by carrying the tools and placing them on the altar. I like to walk three times in a circle around the area clockwise, and on the third time place the tools on the altar.

Hallowing

Stand in the North in the Elhaz stance. Take a moment to center yourself with Baldr and the energy of the Dagaz rune. When you are ready, take the Gandr and trace the Dagaz rune while vibrating its name. Envision the rune glowing yellow and say:

"Gandr í Norðri helga vé þetta ok hindra alla illska."

Turn to the East, trace the Dagaz rune while vibrating its name, envision the rune glowing yellow, and say:

"Gandr í Austri helga vé þetta ok hindra alla illska."

Turn to the South trace the Dagaz rune while vibrating its name, envision the rune glowing yellow, and say:

"Gandr í Suðri helga vé þetta ok hindra alla illska."

Turn to the West, trace the Dagaz rune while vibrating its name, envision the rune glowing yellow, and say:

"Gandr í Vestri helga vé þetta ok hindra alla illska."

Return to the North, look up, trace the Dagaz rune while vibrating its name, envision the rune glowing yellow, and say:
"**Gandr í yfir mér helga vé þetta ok hindra alla illska.**"

Look down, trace the Dagaz rune while vibrating its name, envision the rune glowing yellow, and say:
"**Gandr í undir mér helga vé þetta ok hindra alla illska.**"

With arms outstretched, say:
"As Heimdall guards the Bifröst Bridge, may this *vé* be protected from all unholy or unharmonious wights and ways."

Consecrate Altar

Standing by the altar once again in the North, make the Dagaz rune over it, saying:
"I consecrate this altar, this holy space and all who stand here in the name of Baldr. May our minds be focused and our hearts pure for the working here this day. Hail Baldr! Hail Baldr! Hail Baldr!"

Calling

"Hail Baldr the bright, most beloved of all the Gods, son of Odin and Frigg. Come join us this day in Midgard as we reflect on the light as we head towards darkness. May our sacrifice and your strength guide us both, in the dark days ahead."

This is a good place to tell or read a story about Baldr. Two good ones we've used are "The Slaying of Baldr" in the *Poetic Edda* by Lee M. Hollander, or the story of Baldr in *Myths of the Norsemen* by H.A. Gruber. Either one will help to get everyone focused on Baldr and his importance to us at this time of year.

Charge the mead

Traditionally the Goði (priest) will fill the horn with mead then make the sign of the Dagaz rune over it three times, and while vibrating its name, say:

"We welcome your presence in this holy *vé*, and we offer you sacrifice. We come to you with this gift of our efforts, struggles, and devotion. May this sacrifice aid us, Gods and men alike, against those who would wage war against Asgard or seek to enslave us in mind or body in Midgard."

Hold the horn up high and call out the following:

"Baldr, your light continues to shine in the darkness even after all the countless days you have been held in Hel, pour some of your energy into our holy mead that as we drink we gain your strength to help us in the dark days ahead. Hail Baldr! Hail Baldr! Hail Baldr!"

The Goði then holds up the horn and says:

"Accept our gifts, not as slaves, for we have no master. We bow before no man and yield only to Gods. We offer these gifts not in appeasement, for we stand in good stead with you; but as a sign of our kinship and fellowship."

Sacrifice

At this blót, I like to call everyone to sacrifice by the fire, or to just pour the mead onto the earth so it reaches Baldr in the world below. Each person should raise the horn and hail Baldr in their own words. Then pour some mead into the fire or onto Mother Earth.

Blessing

For this blessing, I like to use a sunwheel carved of wood or made of a thicker paper. I pass it to the first person in the circle and tell them to hold it above their head and reflect upon the power of Baldr. Then pass it to the next person in the circle until it reaches the beginning again, and then say:

"Baldr the bright, your example gives us strength as we walk toward the darkness. May your energy continue to guide us as we walk into the unknown."

At this point, you can burn the sunwheel in the fire or wrap it in a dark cloth. Both signify that Baldr is gone until the day he returns out of darkness. Reflect for a few minutes here in silence.

Closing

"Baldr, your brightness is gone from our eyes, but a spark remains within. You will never be forgotten and together we will face what the darkness brings. We look forward to the day you return. Hail Baldr! Hail Baldr! Hail Baldr!"

Take up the gandr and face North.

Make the sign of Dagaz and vibrate its name.

Turn to the East, make the sign of Dagaz and vibrate its name.

Turn to the South, make the sign of Dagaz and vibrate its name.

Turn to the West, make the sign of Dagaz and vibrate its name.

When you return to the North, say:

"This blót is now ended. It is now time to Feast and Sumbel."

Haymoon/July: Thing Blót

This Blót is held to Tyr. It deals with the law and can also be used to seek justice. At this time of year, legal matters were settled throughout the land, and today we can honor our Ancestors who brought about Anglo-Saxon law by aligning ourselves with man-made law and also laws of nature.

Required Tools

- ∞ Sword
- ∞ Mead
- ∞ Evergreen sprig
- ∞ Bowli
- ∞ Horn
- ∞ Oath ring, if necessary

Have the altar set up beforehand with the ritual tools on it. If you have a larger group, you can have some of them participate by carrying the tools and placing them on the altar. I like to walk three times in a circle around the area clockwise, and on the third time place the tools on the altar.

Hallowing

Start by standing in the North, holding the sword, and standing in the Elhaz stance. Focus on Tyr's energy. Face North, trace the Teiwaz rune while vibrating its name, envision it glowing white, and say:

"Sverd í Norðri helga vé þetta ok hindra alla illska."

Turn to the East, draw the Teiwaz rune while vibrating its name, envision it glowing white, and say:

"Sverd í Austri helga vé þetta ok hindra alla illska."

Turn to the South, draw the Teiwaz rune while vibrating its name, envision it glowing white, and say:

"Sverd í Suðri helga vé þetta ok hindra alla illska."

Turn to the West, draw the Teiwaz rune while vibrating its name, envision it glowing white, and say:

"Sverd í Vestri helga vé þetta ok hindra alla illska."

Return to the North, look up, draw the Teiwaz rune while vibrating its name, envision it glowing white, and say:

"Sverd í yfir mér helga vé þetta ok hindra alla illska."

Look down at the ground, draw the Teiwaz rune while vibrating its name, envision it glowing white, and say:

"Sverd í undir mér vé þetta ok hindra alla illska."

With arms outstretched, say:

"As Heimdall guards the Bifröst Bridge, may this *vé* be protected from all unholy or unharmonious wights and ways."

Consecrate Altar

Standing over the altar, trace the Teiwaz rune three times while vibrating its name. Then say:

"I consecrate this altar, this land and all upon it in the name of Tyr. May our hearts and minds be focused on the law and all it entails. Hail Tyr! Hail Tyr! Hail Tyr!"

Calling

Standing in the Elhaz stance, say:

"Tyr, Tyr, Tyr, we call upon you this day to join us in Midgard. We remember the law. We seek justice and right action. Join us this day and energize us. Hail Tyr!"

Reading

At this time we speak and remind everyone why we are here. Settle any problems and get our heads right for the working to take place here today.

Charge the mead

Traditionally the Goði (priest) will fill the horn with mead, make the sign of the Teiwaz rune three times while vibrating its name, and say:

"We welcome your presence in this holy *vé*, and we offer you sacrifice. We come to you with this gift of our efforts, struggles, and devotion. May this sacrifice aid us, Gods and men alike, against those who would wage war against Asgard or seek to enslave us in mind or body in Midgard."

The Goði then holds up the horn and says:

"Tyr, Tyr, Tyr, pour forth your energy into this horn that it may open our minds to what is right and just. May it strengthen us in our time of need. May we honor the laws of nature and those of men that are honorable and just. Accept our gifts, not as slaves, for we have no master. We bow before no man and yield only to Gods. We offer these gifts not in appeasement, for we stand in good stead with you; but as a sign of our kinship and fellowship."

Lower the horn and look into it as if it is a well and you are seeking knowledge. Then pour a bit into the bowli.

Sacrifice

Allow everyone to approach the altar to raise a horn and speak their minds. Then pour a sacrifice into the bowli.

Blessing

Take the bowli and a sprig and go to each person and sprinkle them with the holy mead while saying a special blessing to each person. For example: "May Tyr bring you justice!" "May right action occur!" "May you honor the law in your actions!"

Group Sacrifice

Standing at the altar, hold up the bowli and say:

"Tyr, we offer you our energies, and together we go forth stronger and wiser in the laws of nature and man. Hail Tyr! Hail Tyr! Hail Tyr!"

Awakening

Before holding this Blót, the group should ask if anyone wants to take an oath. If a member expresses a desire to take an oath—be it to the kindred or to the Gods—he/she must understand the consequences of breaking that oath. This oath will bind all participants together, so it is very important for them to not break their oath. If an oath is to be sworn, the Goði or Chieftain will hold the oath ring out to the oath-taker. He/She will hold onto the offered side and swear the oath they've chosen.

The Goði or Chieftain will say:

"This man/woman has sworn an oath to (insert oath). May the Gods honor and bless their words as we and the Gods hold him/her to it."

Next, the kindred will discuss any unsettled business. The lawspeaker (or chieftain) will address any break of kindred law and sentencing of the offender will be metered out.

Closing

"Tyr, we thank you for your blessings, your strength, and your wisdom. May we all go forth to honor you in word and deed. Hail Tyr! Hail Tyr! Hail Tyr!"

Take up the sword and face North. Make the sign of Teiwaz and vibrate its name.

Turn to the East, make the sign of Teiwaz, and vibrate its name.

Turn to the South, make the sign of Teiwaz, and vibrate its name.

Turn to the West, make the sign of Teiwaz, and vibrate its name.

Returning to the North, say:

"This Blót is now ended!"

(This is a good Blót to follow up with a feast.)

ɦarvest/August: freyfaxi

Freyfaxi marked the time of the harvest festival. We feast in honor of Frey, God of harvest, fertility and properity. In this blót, we thank Frey for the success of our harvest. We ask him to bless us with prosperity and virility in the coming months.

Our Ancestors sacrificed their very best to Frey during the harvest festival, so plan ahead for what you want to sacrifice. It should be something related to a harvest. For example, if you enjoy a good cigar or whiskey, find the very best you can afford. If you choose to bake something instead, use the purest, most unadulterated, organic grains available. If you are in a position where you do not have access to any of those things, then sacrifice your favorite food.

Tools Required

- ൠ Mead or Juice
- ൠ Horn
- ൠ Bowli
- ൠ Evergreen sprig
- ൠ Antler or Gandr (if an antler is not attainable, use a Gandr)

Have the altar set up beforehand with the ritual tools on it. If you have a larger group, you can have some of them participate by carrying the tools and placing them on the altar. I like to walk three times in a circle around the area clockwise, and on the third time place the tools on the altar.

Hallowing

Set up the altar in the west, the direction of Vanaheim. Holding the antler in your sword hand, assume the Elhaz stance with your legs together and arms up in a 45-degree angle. If you cannot use a stag or deer antler, a cardboard or wooden replica will suffice. Take a moment to connect with Ingvi Frey's energy.

When you are ready, face west and trace the Ingwaz rune while vibrating its name. Envision it glowing yellowish-green, and say:

"Hjartar í Vestri helga vé þetta ok hindra alla illska."

Turn to the North, draw the Ingwaz rune while vibrating its name, envision it glowing yellowish-green, and say:

"Hjartar í Norðri, helga vé þetta, ok hindra alla illska."

Turn to the East, draw the Ingwaz rune while vibrating its name, envision it glowing yellowish-green, and say:

"Hjartar í Austri, helga vé þetta, ok hindra alla illska."

Turn to the South, draw the Ingwaz rune while vibrating its name, envision it glowing yellowish-green, and say:

"Hjartar í Suðri, helga vé þetta, ok hindra alla illska."

Return to the West, look up, draw the Ingwaz rune while vibrating its name envision it glowing yellowish-green and say:

"Hjartar í yfir mér helga vé þetta ok hindra alla illska."

Look down, draw the Ingwaz rune while vibrating its name, envision it glowing yellowish-green, and say:

"Hjartar í undir mér helga vé þetta ok hindra alla illska."

With arms outstretched, say:
"As Heimdall guards the Bifröst Bridge, may this *vé* be protected from all unholy or unharmonious wights and ways."

Consecrate Altar

Facing West, stand in the Elhaz position and then say:
"I hallow and make holy this *vé* to the service of Frey. May our minds and wills be hallowed barring all influences deemed unholy or impure to the service of Frey."

Reading/Explanation

You can read the story of Freyfaxi from our mythology, or you can explain the reason you are holding the blót: i.e. to bring strength and growth to the kindred crops, livestock, or yourself. You could also discuss the importance of giving your very best.

Charge the mead

Traditionally the Goði (priest) will fill the horn with mead, then make the sign of the Ingwaz rune over it three times while vibrating its name, and say:
"Frey, we welcome your presence in this holy *vé*, and we offer you sacrifice. We come to you with this gift of our efforts, struggles, and devotion. May this sacrifice aid us, Gods and men alike, against those who would wage war against Asgard or seek to enslave us in mind or body in Midgard."
The Goði then holds up the horn and says:
"Frey, accept our gifts, not as slaves, for we have no master. We bow before no man and yield only to Gods. We offer these gifts not in appeasement, for we stand in good stead with you; but as a sign of our kinship and fellowship."
Face the altar and trace the Ingwaz rune over it three times while vibrating its name. Say the following:

"Frey, God of harvest, prosperity and virility. We thank you for our successful harvest and we ask you to bless us with prosperity and virility in the coming months. Hail Frey! Hail Frey! Hail Frey!"

Sacrifice

Trace the Ingwaz rune over the altar three more times while vibrating "Ingwaz". Reflect upon the harvest you have sown and reaped over the past year. What could you have done better? What did you do successfully? What can you do to be more successful next year? A harvest does not need to be a physical thing; it can be the harvest of ideas or plans that came to fruition. When you are done reflecting, trace the Ingwaz rune over the horn with the antler and say: "Frey, imbue this horn with your essence. Fortify this mead with your gifts of prosperity and virility. Empower us to be successful with our next harvest. Let your boar, Gullinbursti, light our way on the path to success."

Pass the horn and say:

"May Frey grant you prosperity and virility in the coming months. May your next harvest be bountiful and fruitful. May you be successful in your future endeavors."

Pour a small amount of mead in the bowli along with a portion of your sacrifice. When everyone has passed the horn, hold up the bowli and say:

"Frey, we have sacrificed to you our very best to thank you for our harvest."

Blessing

Dip the evergreen sprig in the bowli and bless the celebrants with: "May Frey grant you prosperity and virility in the coming months. May he supply your harvest with sunshine and nourishment. Hail Frey! Hail Frey! Hail Frey! Hail Ingwaz! Hail Ingwaz! Hail Ingwaz!"

Closing

Take up the antler and face West. Make the sign of Ingwaz and vibrate its name.

Turn to the North, make the sign of Ingwaz and vibrate its name. Turn to the East, make the sign of Ingwaz and vibrate its name. Turn to the South, make the sign of Ingwaz and vibrate its name. When you return to the West, say:

"This blót is now ended."

Leave the holy stead. If you have the ability, we suggest you build a bonfire or firepit and place the sacrifices in the center. Light it and reflect upon Frey and the months ahead. If you cannot burn your sacrifice, pour the contents of the bowli and your sacrifice onto the earth in a secluded place.

Shedding/September 20 or 21: Winterfinding, the Autumnal Equinox

On the 20th or 21st of Shedding/September, we hold a blót to Odin and we ask for the gifts of his wisdom and inspiration to see us through the coming winter.

At this time of year, our ancestors would take inventory of their supplies and the yield of the last harvest of the year. If they had a successful harvest and planned wisely for the winter, they would survive. If they had a poor harvest or were unwise in their winter planning, some kin could perish during the barren winter months. They would pray to Odin for his wisdom to make the right choices over the winter months, and for inspiration to make ends meet when things seemed bleak and hopeless.

In our day and age, most of us do not face the harsh conditions and the life-or-death decisions our ancestors had to endure. Our circumstances are not as dire, but our planning and decisions do affect our lives and our families. So in this blót we reflect upon the trials and tribulations our ancestors endured. We ask Odin to guide our decisions with his wisdom and to inspire us when times are tough.

Tools Required

ᚱ Mead or Juice

ᚳᚱ Horn

ᚳᚱ Bowli

ᚳᚱ Evergreen sprig

ᚳᚱ Sunwheel

ᚳᚱ Gandr

ᚳᚱ The Ansuz, Laguz, and Uruz runes from your set

Have the altar set up beforehand with the ritual tools on it. If you have a larger group, you can have some of them participate by carrying the tools and placing them on the altar. I like to walk three times in a circle around the area clockwise, and on the third time place the tools on the altar.

Hallowing

Set everything upon the altar. Take the Gandr, face North, and trace the Ansuz rune while vibrating its name. Envision it glowing blue and say:

"Gandr í Norðri helga vé þetta ok hindra alla illska."

Turn to the East, trace the Ansuz rune while vibrating its name, envision it glowing blue, and say:

"Gandr í Austri helga vé þetta ok hindra alla illska."

Turn to the South, trace the Ansuz rune while vibrating its name, envision it glowing blue, and say:

"Gandr í Suðri helga vé þetta ok hindra alla illska."

Turn to the West, trace the Ansuz rune while vibrating its name, envision it glowing blue, and say:

"Gandr í Vestri helga vé þetta ok hindra alla illska."

Return to the North, look up, trace the Ansuz rune while vibrating its name, envision it glowing blue, and say:

"Gandr í yfir mér helga vé þetta ok hindra alla illska."

Look down, draw the Ansuz rune while vibrating its name, envision it glowing blue, and say:

"Gandr í undir mér helga vé þetta ok hindra alla illska."

With arms outstretched, say: "As Heimdall guards the Bifröst Bridge, may this *vé* be protected from all unholy or unharmonious wights and ways."

Consecrate Altar

"Odin, hallow and hold this holy vé and prevent all evil from entering!"

With the Gandr, trace the Ansuz rune over the altar three times while vibrating "Ansuz". Turn to each celebrant, touch their forehead with the Gandr, and say:

"May Odin the far-wanderer, master of inspiration, winner of the runes, Göndlir-bearer of the magic wand, grant you the wisdom and inspiration you seek."

Put the Gandr down and pick up the sunwheel. Raise it over your head and say:

"Sigfather – Victory Father, let the light of your wisdom and inspiration shine through the darkness and enlighten us in the days to come."

Focus on the sunwheel and feel the energy of the sun, along with Odin's energy, flow from it to you. Hand the sunwheel to each celebrant and say:

"May Sviðurr's wisdom shine upon you in the dark days ahead. Hail Odin! Hail Sigfather! Hail Sviðurr!"

Reading

Reflect upon what our ancestors had to do at this time: they would take stock of all their resources and plan their meals for the next several months. If their harvest was poor or they failed to plan correctly, their meals would be meager; family memebers would go hungry and possibly die from starvation. At this point you may want to read a section of the Havamal, sagas, or Eddas that you feel is appropriate. You may want to consider "The Lay of Vafþrúðnir" or "The Lay of Grímnir".

Charge the mead

Traditionally the Goði (priest) will fill the horn with mead then make the sign of the Ansuz rune over it three times, and while vibrating its name, say:

"We welcome your presence in this holy *vé*, and we offer you sacrifice. We come to you with this gift of our efforts, struggles, and devotion. May this sacrifice aid us, Gods and men alike, against those who would wage war against Asgard or seek to enslave us in mind or body in Midgard."

The Goði then holds up the horn and says:

"Accept our gifts, not as slaves, for we have no master. We bow before no man and yield only to Gods. We offer these gifts not in appeasement, for we stand in good stead with you; but as a sign of our kinship and fellowship."

Sacrifice

Turn to the altar and take up the three runes (Ansuz, Laguz, and Uruz). Hold the Ansuz rune over the horn and vibrate its name three times. With your fingernail, gently scrape a tiny portion of the rune into your horn. Do the same for the other two runes. *(If you have constructed your runes of a dense material such as stone, you may need to use something other than your fingernail to scrape the rune.)*

Then turn to the altar and call to Odin: "Odin, All-Father, imbue this mead with the gifts of your wisdom and inspiration."

Then vibrate: "Ansuz, Laguz, Uruz."

Pour out your sacrifice then pass the horn and say: "May Odin's wisdom and inspiration guide you."

The other celebrants accept the horn, and repeat the scraping of the runes and the vibration of the runes. When the horn has been passed and the bowli has been filled, hold it up over the altar and say:

"Odin, we thank you for your gifts and your guidance in the days ahead."

Blessing

Dip the sprig in the bowli and bless each celebrant, saying:
"May Odin's wisdom and inspiration guide you through the winter months."

Then vibrate "Ansuz, Laguz, Uruz," and call out "Hail Odin! Hail Odin! Hail Odin!"

Closing

Take up the gandr and face North. Make the sign of Ansuz and vibrate its name.

Turn to the East, make the sign of Ansuz and vibrate its name.

Turn to the South, make the sign of Ansuz and vibrate its name.

Turn to the West, make the sign of Ansuz and vibrate its name.

When you return to the North, say:

"This blót is now ended."

After everyone has left the area, return and pour the bowli out onto the earth.

Hear thou, Loddfáfnir, and heed it well:
Learn it, 'twill lend thee strength;
Follow it, 'twill further thee;
If wrong was done thee let they wrong be known,
And fall on thy foes straightaway.
-The Hávámal

Ɖunting/October: Disablót

Valgard Murray

The Importance of the Disir

The Disir were originally the deified female ancestors of the family and clan. They were, and are, the ruling Matriarch Mothers that were worshipped before the coming of the Patriarch Aesir Gods to Northern Europe. Freya is the great Vanadís, heading the Disir, one of Her titles being *Drottning disanna*, Queen of the Disir.

In late Heathen times in the North, the term *Dis* and *Disir* came to mean any Scandinavian Goddess or Goddesses, but the Disir remain today within the Ásatrú Folk Soul as fate Goddesses ruling over fertility, the increase of one's well being, and the luck of the clan and family. The Disir were worshipped in a sacrificial rite called the *disablót,* which involves much ceremonial drinking, feasting, and storytelling of the deeds of favorite ancestors. The family celebrates the great disablót on *Vetrnaeter/Winter Nights,* which falls on the second Friggsday of October. However, the Disir may and should be honored at other times as well with sacrificial offerings and blótar, as it pays to court their services and protection for the preservation of the family and clan. The disablót is usually carried out by the head woman or mother of the clan before an outdoor altar or indoor *stalli.*

If there are no women present, a Goði or male head of the clan may perform the rite. The Disir are of great importance to every individual and the clan worship, and no matter what High God or Goddess one has chosen, the Disir are on a higher level, because they are up close and personal to us all on a daily basis.

The Disir are pictured as beautiful spirit Goddesses who reside at the homestead with the mother and housewife. They may bestow their blessings on the relationship that the family and clan maintains with them. At the blót feast, one should place three extra plates at one's table to honor them, and drink many toasts to them during the evening rites. I personally believe that it is the Disir who surround you at your time of death and guide your spirit to the Folk Soul and the halls of your ancestors. With that being said, it is best to live a virtuous life.

It is important to know that the concept and worship of the Disir is where the Christians got their concept of a *guardian angel*. Since the Jewish Bible only makes references to archangels, who are in essence the "killer angels" of Jehovah, the "archangels" are shown as male, and the "guardian angels" are shown as female.

1) Perform the Hamarsign at the altar.

2) Facing North, making the Elhaz rune with your body, and say: "Hail ye holy ides, Disir of the hold, you whole and holy kindred. You are known by many names, you great mothers of our folk who ever drive us forward to more daring deeds, and to more fruitful fields and orchards. Hail, you spae wives, you wonderfully womanly wights all, we call out to you and honor you all in the ancient manner of the Ásatrú. Tonight we name the Winter Nights and call forth the Disir of the kindred. You are known by many names." Facing North, pour ale or mead into the horn and holding it aloft, saying: "We give to you this offering, blended with awe and devotion to you, O Mighty Mothers old and new."

3) The Gyðia then pours a portion of the offering for ach participant in turn, and they individually pay their respects to the ancestors. She then returns to the altar and pours the remaining mead into the *bowli,* clockwise blesses the assembled with an evergreen twig dipped in the mead, and says; "I give you the blessings of the Disir and all the holy mothers.

4) The Gyðia then blesses the altar three times with the sprig, declaring: "To all the Disir and all your holy tides."

5) The Gyðia then takes the remaining mead in the bowli and offers it to the soil from which the sprig was taken, silently saying thank you all holy beings. She then says; "Holy mothers of men/holy mothers of women/Wyrd daughters of Odinn/to you we give this sacrifice."

6) The Gyðia then faces north again, making the Elhaz rune with her body, and says: "From these nights till the twelfth night of Yule, the walls between the world of the Disir all dead, and we the living here, grows thinner. May the wisdom of these wise women, all loving, become known to all here tonight. This blot has ended."

The feast in honor of the ancestors is then brought forward and shared by the kindred. Shortly thereafter, the kindred gathers around the fire for sumbel and ritual toasting.

I personally have photos and personal effects of my ancestors present on my *stalli*, and leave offerings of flowers when in season to them. I also leave a shot glass with whiskey to the Alfar (male ancestors) on the stalli with my deepest respects.

Fogmoon/November 11: Odin Blót and Feast of Einherjar

This blót is done to bring to mind the chosen of Odin, those warriors who prepare for the great battle ahead. We use this blót to honor those heroes of the folk who have done something to make them worthy of a place in Odin's hall. It is traditional to hold a great feast and raise many horns. *Hail the Einherjar! Hail Odin's chosen!*

Required Tools

- Thor's hammer
- Gandr
- Mead
- Evergreen sprig
- Bowli
- Horn

Have the altar set up beforehand with the ritual tools on it. If you have a larger group, you can have some of them participate by carrying the tools and placing them on the altar. I like to walk three times in a circle around the area clockwise, and on the third time place the tools on the altar.

Hallowing

Standing in the North at the altar, hold the Gandr in one hand and a large Thor's hammer in the other. Starting in the North, trace the Ansuz rune while vibrating its name. Envision it glowing blue, and call out:

"Gandr/hamar í Norðri, helga vé þetta, ok hindra alla illska."

Turn to the East, trace the Ansuz rune while vibrating its name, envision it glowing blue, and say:

"Gandr/hamar í Austri, helga vé þetta, ok hindra alla illska"

Turn to the South, trace the Ansuz rune while vibrating its name, envision it glowing blue, and say:

"Gandr/hamar í Suðri, helga vé þetta, ok hindra alla illska."

Turn to the West, trace the Ansuz rune while vibrating its name, envision it glowing blue, and say:

"Gandr/hamar í Vestri, helga vé þetta, ok hindra alla illska."

Return to the North, look up, trace the Ansuz rune while vibrating its name, envision it glowing blue, say:

"Gandr/hamar í yfir mér helga vé þetta ok hindra alla illska."

Look down, trace the Ansuz rune while vibrating its name, envision it glowing blue, and say:

"Gandr/hamar í undir mér helga vé þetta ok hindra alla illska."

With arms outstretched, say:

"As Heimdall guards the Bifröst Bridge, may this *vé* be protected from all unholy or unharmonious wights and ways."

Consecrate Altar

Stand in front of the altar. Using the Gandr, trace the Ansuz rune in the air while vibrating its name three times, then say:

"I consecrate and make holy this land and all upon it in the name of Odin. May all you who seek to do us harm hide in fear as we call upon Odin and his chosen to join us here this day. As Heimdall guards the Bifröst Bridge, may this *vé* be protected from all unholy or unharmonious wights and ways. Hail Odin! Hail the Einherjar! Hail the Chosen!"

Calling

Stand in the North in the Elhaz stance, holding the hammer and Gandr, and say:

"Odin, All-Father, we call upon you and your chosen, the Einherjar, to join us here this day to share in the blót and feast as in your hall. May those here be deemed worthy to raise a horn and be heard and counted as true folk here in Midgard."

Reading/Explanation

At this point you should read a story about a hero of the folk, or explain that the Einherjar are those who dedicated their life to Odin in hopes of becoming one of his chosen who reside in Valhalla and fight all day and feast all night, preparing for Ragnarök. These warriors, it is said, are taken at the time of their life when they are best and known to have done deeds worthy to sit in Odin's hall.

Charge Horn

Traditionally the Goði (priest) will fill the horn with mead, then make the sign of the Ansuz rune over it three times while vibrating its name, and then say:

"We welcome your presence in this holy *vé*, and we offer you sacrifice. We come to you with this gift of our efforts, struggles, and devotion. May this sacrifice aid us, Gods and men alike, against those who would wage war against Asgard or seek to enslave us in mind or body in Midgard."

The Goði then holds up the horn and says:

"Accept our gifts, not as slaves, for we have no master. We bow before no man and yield only to Gods. We offer these gifts not in appeasement, for we stand in good stead with you; but as a sign of our kinship and fellowship."

Stand at the altar with a horn of mead raised high, and call out to Odin to place his energy into the horn:

"Odin, those gathered here this day ask you to bless us with your strength and wisdom, so that we will be prepared for battle in the days ahead. Pour forth your energy into this sacred mead, so that as it touches our lips we become inspired to fight in word and deed for folk and family."

Sacrifice

Allow everyone to approach the altar, raise a horn to Odin and the Einherjar, then pour a sacrifice into the bowli. Hold the bowli up high and offer the group's combined energies to Odin and the Einherjar.

"Odin, All-Father, warriors of the Einherjar, we offer you this sacrifice, our very best to strengthen the Gods and Man alike. May we all prepare for battle together, both here in Midgard and Valhalla. Hail the chosen of Odin! Hail the Einherjar! Hail Odin!"

Blessing

Carrying the Gandr and the larger Thor's hammer, walk to everyone in the group. With your arms crossed, making the Gebo rune, touch the left shoulder with the hammer and the right with the Gandr while saying: "By Gandr and hammer, may your deeds be judged worthy of Valhalla."

Closing

"All-Father Odin, warriors of Valhalla, ancestors of old, we thank you for your blessings here this day. May you watch proudly as we go forth with newfound strength and wisdom. We wish you well as you find your way back to Valhalla."

Take up the hammer/Gandr and face North. Make the sign of Ansuz and vibrate its name.

Turn to the East, make the sign of Ansuz and vibrate its name.

Turn to the South, make the sign of Ansuz and vibrate its name.

Turn to the West, make the sign of Ansuz and vibrate its name.

When you return to the North, say: "This blót is now ended."

Yule/December 20 or 21: Winter Solstice

The following is a blót to Thor. We have been taught that this is when he breaks winter's back and we start the journey back towards the light (spring).

Required Tools

- ᛉ Thor's hammer
- ᛉ Mead
- ᛉ Evergreen sprig
- ᛉ Bowli
- ᛉ Horn

Have the altar set up beforehand with the ritual tools on it. If you have a larger group, you can have some of them participate by carrying the tools and placing them on the altar. I like to walk three times in a circle around the area clockwise, and on the third time place the tools on the altar.

Hallowing

Standing in the North, using a large Thor's hammer and standing in the Elhaz stance with arms raised, trace the Thurisaz rune while vibrating its name, and say:

"Hamar í Norðri helga vé þetta, ok hindra alla illska."

Turn to the East, trace the Thurisaz rune while vibrating its name, envision the rune glowing red, and say:
"Hamar í Austri helga vé þetta, ok hindra alla illska."

Turn to the South, trace the Thurisaz rune while vibrating its name, envision the rune glowing red, and say:
"Hamar í Suðri helga vé þetta, ok hindra alla illska."

Turn to the West, trace the Thurisaz rune while vibrating its name, envision the rune glowing red, and say:
"Hamar í Vestri helga vé þetta, ok hindra alla illska."

Return to the North, look up, trace the Thurisaz rune while vibrating its name, envision the rune glowing red, and say:
"Hamar í yfir mér helga vé þetta ok hindra alla illska."

Look down, trace the Thurisaz rune while vibrating its name, envision the rune glowing red, and say:
"Hamar í undir mér vé þetta ok hindra alla illska."

Place the Thor's hammer on the altar and, with arms outstretched, say:
"As Heimdall guards the Bifröst Bridge, may this *vé* be protected from all unholy or unharmonious wights and ways."

Consecrate Altar

Once back in the North in front of the altar, say the following:
"I consecrate this altar, this holy space, and all upon it in the name of the mighty Thor. May our hearts and minds be pure for the workings here this day."

Calling

Standing in the North, call out the following:

"Mighty Thor, defender of the Gods and Man, we call upon you this day to join us in Midgard, to break the back of winter, and march with us as we travel from the darkness into the light. Hail Thor! Hail red-bearded brother! Hail Mjölnir's Wielder!"

(Note: You could have everyone present call out and hail Thor by a different name.)

Explanation/Story

We tell a story here, or explain what the blót is about, so that everyone will be focused and thinking about the same thing, allowing the energy raised to be more powerful. For example, you could say:

"It is at this time of year when the mighty Thor breaks winter's back, allowing us to head once again towards the warmth and light of spring, and out of darkness. Think of what is holding you back, and how you can break through it with the strength of Thor. What are you willing to sacrifice in order to gain his strength?"

Charging the mead

Traditionally the Goði (priest) will fill the horn with mead, then make the sign of the Thurisaz rune over it three times while vibrating its name, and say:

"We welcome your presence in this holy *vé*, and we offer you sacrifice. We come to you with this gift of our efforts, struggles, and devotion. May this sacrifice aid us, Gods and men alike, against those who would wage war against Asgard or seek to enslave us in mind or body in Midgard."

The Goði then holds up the horn and says:

"Accept our gifts, not as slaves, for we have no master. We bow before no man and yield only to Gods. We offer these gifts not in appeasement, for we stand in good stead with you; but as a sign of our kinship and fellowship."

Standing at the altar and holding a horn of mead, call out for Thor to bless the mead with his energy.

"Mighty Thor, pour forth your energy into this holy mead so that it will provide us with the strength needed to overcome all that which is holding us back. Together we will break winter's back and march from the darkness into the light. Strengthen us now, Brother, as you strengthened our ancestors in their time of need. Hail Thor! Hail Thor! Hail Thor!"

Lower the horn in front of you and look into the mead, and feel the power of Thor as it enters the horn. *(There have been times I could hardly hold on to the horn, as the energy was so great.)*

Sacrifice

Allow each person to approach the altar and raise the horn to Thor, speaking in their own words, and then pour a sacrifice into the bowli. As you hand them the horn, say:

"May Thor give you his strength and energy this day."

Blessing

Hold the bowli in front of you and say:

"Mighty Thor, may our combined sacrifice bring strength to us all. This holy bowli contains our very best. Not of blood as in the days of old, but from our hearts and minds. We freely give all we have to offer."

Carrying the bowli around the circle and using the sprig dipped in the holy mead, bless each person by sprinkling them with the mead and giving them a personal blessing. For example:

"May Thor's strength be seen in your actions." "May you find the strength of Thor within." "May Thor's strength enable you to do great things."

Rune Pull

During this ritual, we do a rune pull. Each person pulls three runes from the kindred rune bag while reflecting on a question they have asked the Norns. Before beginning, tell everyone to think of the question they have. Reflect in silence for a few minutes, and then say,

"Holy Norns! Urð, Verðandi, Skuld! Open the runic paths and allow me to find the answer I seek."

Let everyone make their pick. Replace the runes in a bag and go from person to person, and once everyone is done, say,

"Holy Norns, we thank you for your guidance this day."

Sunwheel Lighting (Optional Step)

Some kindreds like to pass a hand-made sunwheel around the group, and then light it on the fire to symbolize the sun getting brighter and winters back being broken. If you decide to do this step, make a sunwheel from paper/cardboard/straw/twigs and pass it around the circle while chanting,

"Thor has broken winter's back and we now watch as the sun comes back."

After everyone has touched the sunwheel, burn it in the fire pit, still chanting as the fire flares up. Some people like to jump over the fire for luck; others do so for the purification aspects of the smoke as spoken of in our lore.

Group Sacrifice

Stand at the altar with the bowli raised high above your head and say,

"Mighty Thor, Gods and Goddesses of my ancestors, may our sacrifice this day strengthen us all and hasten the return of the light and life. We sacrifice this today to Mother Earth to strengthen her and the land wights in the days ahead." Then pour the contents of the bowli onto Mother Earth.

Closing

Stand in front of the altar and say: "Thor, Thor, Thor! We thank you for your blessings. We thank you for your strength. May our paths cross once again. Fare well on your journey homeward."

Take up the hammer and face North. Make the sign of Thurisaz and vibrate its name.

Turn to the East, make the sign of Thurisaz and vibrate its name.

Turn to the South, make the sign of Thurisaz and vibrate its name.

Turn to the West, make the sign of Thurisaz and vibrate its name. When you return to the North, say:

"This blót is now ended. Now we shall feast and sumbel. Hail Thor, Hail Thor, Hail Thor!"

Yule/December 31: Twelfth Night

During the first eleven days of our Yuletide celebration, which begins on the 19th, we feast and reflect upon the past year. On the twelfth night we prepare for the coming year by asking for Odin's guidance, Thor's protection, and Frey's gift of fruitful abundance. You may also choose to make a New Year's resolution by swearing an oath on Frey's boar Gullinbursti.

Have the altar set up beforehand with the ritual tools on it. If you have a larger group, you can have some of them participate by carrying the tools and placing them on the altar. I like to walk three times in a circle around the area clockwise, and on the third time place the tools on the altar.

Before we begin our walk onto sacred land, take a few minutes to review the past year. Ask yourself what you need to work on in the coming year. What aspects of yourself do you want to change? Will you swear an oath on Gullinbursti as a New Years resolution?

Required Tools

- ෴ Gandr
- ෴ Large Thor's hammer
- ෴ Horn
- ෴ Mead or juice
- ෴ Evergreen sprig
- ෴ An oath ring or a statue of Gullinbursti
- ෴ Set of runes (use a kindred set if this is in a group setting, or a personal set if this is a solitary blót)

Hallowing

Start in the north facing the altar. Holding the Gandr in one hand and a Thor's hammer in the other, assume the Elhaz stance. Take a moment to draw in Odin and Thor's energy. When you are ready, trace the Ansuz rune with the Gandr while vibrating its name, and envision it glowing pale blue. Then trace the Thurisaz rune with the hammer while vibrating its name. Envision it glowing red, and then say:

"Gandr/Hamar í Norðri helga vé þetta, ok hindra alla illska."

Turn to the East, trace the Ansuz rune with the Gandr while vibrating its name, and envision it glowing pale blue. Trace the Thurisaz rune with the hammer while vibrating its name, envision the rune glowing red, and say:

"Gandr/Hamar í Austri helga vé þetta, ok hindra alla illska."

Turn to the South, trace the Ansuz rune with the Gandr while vibrating its name, and envision it glowing pale blue. Trace the Thurisaz rune with the hammer while vibrating its name, envision the rune glowing red, and say:

"Gandr/Hamar í Suðri helga vé þetta, ok hindra alla illska."

Turn to the West trace the Ansuz rune with the Gandr while vibrating its name, and envision it glowing pale blue. Trace the Thurisaz rune with the hammer while vibrating its name, envision the rune glowing red, and say:

"Gandr/Hamar í Vestri helga vé þetta, ok hindra alla illska."

Return to the North, look up, trace the Ansuz rune with the Gandr while vibrating its name, and envision it glowing pale blue. Trace the Thurisaz rune with the hammer while vibrating its name, envision the rune glowing red, and say:

"Gandr/Hamar í yfir mér helga vé þetta ok hindra alla illska."

Look down, trace the Ansuz rune with the Gandr while vibrating its name and envision it glowing pale blue. Trace the Thurisaz rune with the hammer while vibrating its name, envision the rune glowing red, and say:

"Gandr/Hamar í undir mér helga vé þetta ok hindra alla illska."

With arms outstretched, say:

"As Heimdall guards the Bifröst Bridge, may this *vé* be protected from all unholy or unharmonious wights and ways."

Consecrate Altar

As you return to the north, stand in front of the altar. Using the Gandr, make the sign of Ansuz over the altar. Then trace the Thurisaz rune with the hammer and say:

"I hallow this altar, this land, and those upon it in the names of Odin and Thor. May our hearts and minds be pure for the workings here today. Hail Odin, Hail Thor! Hail Odin, Hail Thor! Hail Odin, Hail Thor!"

Invocation

"Odin, All-Father, we ask you to join us here in Midgard as we offer you sacrifice today. We ask that you guide us with your wisdom in this coming year. Thor, protector of Midgard, we ask you to protect us and our kin throughout the new year."

Address the Gathered Folk

"We gather this Twelfth day of Yule to ask for the Gods' guidance, protection and gift of fertility in the coming year. Over the past eleven days we have reviewed the previous year. We have learned from both our successes and failures, and ask for the Gods' blessings moving forward."

Charge the Mead

Traditionally the Goði (priest) will fill the horn with mead, then make the sign of the Ansuz rune and the Thurisaz rune over it three times while vibrating their names, and say:

"We welcome your presence in this holy *vé*, and we offer you sacrifice. We come to you with this gift of our efforts, struggles, and devotion. May this sacrifice aid us, Gods and men alike, against those who would wage war against Asgard or seek to enslave us in mind or body in Midgard."

Standing in front of the altar, raise the horn above your head and say:

"All-Father, we ask for your wisdom and guidance in the coming year. Help us make the correct decisions when we are uncertain. Thor, guardian of Midgard, we ask for you to shield our families, our kin, and ourselves from harm. Fill this sacred mead with your combined energy so that when it passes our lips, your power will flow through our bodies, giving us that which we seek. In turn we sacrifice to you. Hail Odin, Hail Thor! Hail Odin, Hail Thor! Hail Odin, Hail Thor! Accept our gifts, not as slaves, for we have no master. We bow before no man and yield only to Gods. We offer these gifts not in appeasement, for we stand in good stead with you; but as a sign of our kinship and fellowship."

Lower the horn in front of you until you see or feel the combined energy of Odin and Thor flowing into the horn. Drink of the mead and then pour some into the bowli as a sacrifice.

Sacrifice

Invite each person to approach the altar and accept the mead, and say: "May the All-Father's wisdom and Thor's protection be with you throughout the new year."

Give each person a chance to raise the horn and say something in their own words. They can then take a sip and pour a small portion into the bowli.

Optional: If a member wants to make a New Year's resolution by swearing an oath on Gullinbursti, now would be the time. Make sure they are fully aware of the circumstances of breaking their oath. This should be discussed well in advance with each participant, because this oath will bind not only the individual, but to everyone participating in the blót.

If this is to be done, the person taking the oath will approach the altar. The Goði will hold out the oath ring or the statue of Gullinbursti. The oath taker will hold it with his/her sword hand and say:

"I, (state your kindred name), swear on Gullinbursti that I will (state your resolution). Hail Frey! Hail Frey! Hail Frey!"

Blessing

Hold the bowli in front of you and say:

"May our combined sacrifices strengthen both the Gods and Man alike. Let the power of Gebo strengthen us all."

Take the sprig and bowli and walk around to each person. Dip the sprig into the bowli and bless each person, saying:

"May Odin guide you in the days ahead, and may Thor protect you and your loved ones."

After everyone has received a blessing, return to the altar. Hold the bowli above your head and say:

"May the combined energies of the Gods and Man strengthen us all in our time of need, and may each of us be blessed with a fruitful year ahead."

Pour the contents of the bowli onto the Earth, trace the Ingwaz rune, and say:

"Today we have asked for Odin and Thor to bless us in the days ahead. In turn we offer up our sacrifice to Frey, God of fertility, for a bountiful harvest in the coming year. Hail Frey! Hail Frey! Hail Frey!"

Rune Pull

Return to the altar and take up the runes. Meditate for a moment on each of the twenty-four runes and then say: "Urðr, Verðandi, Skuld, open the runic streams to give us a glimpse of the coming year."

Reach into the rune bag and pull out one rune. That rune represents what to expect in the following month. Pull out another rune and continue until you have drawn twelve runes in total. Tyrsoak pulls two runes for each month and Faolchú only pulls one; you should experiment and see which way you prefer. Examine them in the order you pulled them. You should have someone record your results so you can analyze it to prepare for the coming months.

An example of a rune pull:

January	ᚠ ᚱ	July	ᚨ ᛗ
February	ᚢ ᚦ	August	ᛒ ᛏ
March	ᚨ ᚱ	September	ᛋ ᛦ
April	ᚲ ᚷ	October	ᛦ ᛋ
May	ᚹ ᚾ	November	ᛂ ᛁ
June	ᛗ ᛜ	December	ᛏ ᚺ

Closing

Stand in front of the altar in the Elhaz stance and say: "Odin, All-Father, we thank you for your guidance that keeps us on the true path of the Old Ways. Thor, thank you for your protection and strength. We wish you well as you head homeward."

Face the North, take up the Gandr and hammer, and make the sign of Ansuz and Thurisaz while vibrating their names.

Turn to the East, make the sign of Ansuz and Thurisaz and vibrate their names.

Turn to the South, make the sign of Ansuz and Thurisaz and vibrate their names.

Turn to the West, make the sign of Ansuz and Thurisaz and vibrate their names.

Return to the North, and say: "This blót is now ended!"

Other Rites

Rites of Passage Used by the Guardians of Othala

These rites of passage into the Guardians of Othala Kindred begin when someone decides they wish to start on the path of Ásatrú. The rite of self-profession is between that person and the Gods and Goddesses. With this rite, they are making a commitment to follow the path of Ásatrú.

The rite of fostering is one in which a full member who has acquired a store of knowledge about our way of life decides to undertake helping someone new to our way of life learn some of the basic tenets of Ásatrú. Only someone who has shown they are willing to put this knowledge into action should be chosen as a fosterer. Both should be committed to helping others grow in the Old Way. Many choose to bear the name of their fosterer (i.e. Williamsson) to show the bond and level of commitment on both sides.

The rite of profession to the kindred happens when someone decides they wish to become a full member of our kindred or family, and the kindred feels that the person would be a good addition. The person needs a unanimous vote to be accepted in. During the person's fostering, they are watched and questioned to see if they are truly committed to our way of life. In addition, a meeting is required with all kindred members before a vote is taken. Our oath speaks for itself. Once taken, a bond is forged that will endure all hardships and will reach throughout the nine worlds. We are family—we are one.

Rite of Self-Profession

ଓ Stand before the altar and meditate for a few minutes on the purpose of the ritual. Then take up a vessel (bowli) of pure water and say: "Odin, Thor, and Tyr, may this pure and holy water here cleanse from me all alien stain, that my mind and heart with our Gods and Goddesses shall remain."

- ◌ Set the bowli down, dip the fingers of the sword hand in the water, and make a fist.

- ◌ Touch your forehead and say: "Odin, give me wisdom and inspiration."

- ◌ Touch your heart and say: "Baldr, give me boldness tempered with goodness."

- ◌ Touch your left shoulder and say: "Frey, give me plenty and joy."

- ◌ Touch right shoulder and say: "Thor, give me might and main."

- ◌ Having made the hammer sign in this fashion, address the Deity to which you feel especially close (in words of your own choosing). Close by saying the our Kindred Oath.

Rite of Fostering

Sponsor *(to Goði)*: "I have one here who shows within himself the spark of divinity as a true follower of the Way. It is my duty to sponsor this one and to nurture that divinity for the betterment of the kindred."

Goði: "Are you willing to bear his Troth and actions as your own?"

Sponsor: "I am."

Goði to Associate: "Do you, young one, understand the level of commitment being undertaken by this true follower of the Way?"

Associate: "I do."

Goði: "Are you ready to match this commitment as you take your first steps on the path of your ancestors?"

Associate: "I am."

Goði: "Then as you stand before the Guardians of Othala kindred, your ancestors and the Gods and Goddesses of the Folk, you shall hereby be known by the name of *(associate's chosen Ásatrú name)* and be a provisional member of the Guardians of Othala. Walk in rightness, for you are a reflection of all that we hold to be holy. So shall it be. Go with the Gods and Goddesses."

Rite of Profession to the Kindred

Profession in Ásatrú is a major and lifelong commitment to our Gods and Goddesses, our ancestors, and the kindred Folk. This is not something that should be taken lightly. Only those who are true to the ways of our Folk need to travel down this road. The rite of profession is unlike any other rite. It consists primarily of an exchange between the initiate and the Goði. It can be performed for an individual or a group of initiates. The Goði pours the sacred mead and calls on the Gods and Goddesses. Then the Goði faces the gathered Folk.

Sponsor *(to Goði)*: "I have one here who is young in the way of our folk, but worthy, and I wish to bring them into the kindred."

Goði: "Send them forward." *(Initiate steps before Goði.)* "Who are you?" *(If there is more than one initiate, the Goði will speak to each in turn.) The initiate gives their common name, or a name by which they choose to be known.*

Goði: "What do you seek?" *The initiate responds in their own words that which they seek: i.e. to be bonded into the fellowship of Ásatrú and the kindred.*

Goði: "Have you studied the ways of our Folk, and do you freely choose to follow our way?"

Initiate: "I do."

The Chieftain or sponsor produces the Oath Ring and gives it to the Goði. Initiate grasps opposite side of Oath Ring.

Initiate: I will be true to the faith of our ancestors and to the (name of your kindred). I will honor all my fellows in the kindred with my loyalty and my trust. My arm will be their arm. My voice will be their voice. My weapon shall be their weapon. I will extend to them my hand in help and in friendship. I will stand by them in peace as well as in war, in plenty and in poverty. Wrong done to them will be avenged. Good done to them will be rewarded. So I swear by the powers that order the worlds, by my forefathers and clan, and by my own name. Shall I break this oath, may I be spurned by all and bear the name of oath-breaker, and may my weapons fail me in time of dire need."

Goði: "So may it be written by the Norns." *(The Goði dips his fingers in the sacred mead and traces a sunwheel on the initiate's forehead.)* "May Odin give you wisdom."

Initiate: "Hail Odin!"

Goði: *(Traces a sunwheel on the initiate's solar plexus.)* "May Baldr give you boldness."

Initiate: "Hail Baldr!"

Goði: *(Traces a sunwheel on the initiate's left shoulder.)* "May Frey give you prosperity."

Initiate: "Hail Frey."

Goði: *(Traces a sunwheel on the initiate's right shoulder.)* "May Thor give you strength."

Initiate: "Hail Thor."

Goði: I welcome you into the fellowship of (name of your kindred)."

Ḋammer Ritual

The hammer ritual is done when you purchase or make a Thor's hammer, and you wish to give it part of your essence or soul and bring it to life. This hammer then becomes a part of you, and is like a great family heirloom which has a lot of value, as well as a very powerful tool which can be used for various purposes. It is also considered bad luck to allow someone to gain possession of your hammer, as it does contain a part of your essence after the hammer ritual. Have a name for your hammer ready prior to the ritual and do not share it with anyone. To do this ritual, it is best to have the following laid out prior to starting:

- ◌ A larger Thor's hammer made of wood or paper
- ◌ The Thor's hammer you made or purchased
- ◌ White cloth or piece of white paper (you can mark runes or symbols on this)
- ◌ Dark cloth or dark piece of paper
- ◌ 12″ piece of twine, thread, or something similar
- ◌ Source of light such as a candle, light, sunlight, or even a picture of the sun if you are unable to have access to any of the others
- ◌ A pin or razor blade
- ◌ Small table or counter or property bin to place all the materials on. Place it in the middle of the room or area you are using for the ritual. Set the Thor's hammer in the middle of the white cloth or paper.

Part 1

It is best to do this ritual in the early evening. Take a few minutes to clear your head of all thoughts other than the ritual. Picture Thor, focus on your hammer, or on the runes. Once you feel you are ready, start in the North, standing in the Elhaz stance with the larger Thor's hammer.

Hallowing

Speak while moving to each of the four directions, ending up back in the North in front of the table you are using as an altar. Trace the Kenaz rune while vibrating its name, and say:

"Hamar í Norði, helga vé þetta, ok hindra alla illska."

Turn to the East, trace the Kenaz rune while vibrating its name, and say:
"Hamar í Austri, helga vé þetta, ok hindra alla illska."

Turn to the South, trace the Kenaz rune while vibrating its name, and say:
"Hamar í Suðri, helga vé þetta, ok hindra alla illska."

Turn to the West, trace the Kenaz rune while vibrating its name, and say:
"Hamar í Vestri, helga vé þetta, ok hindra alla illska."

Return to the North, look up, trace the Kenaz rune while vibrating its name, and say:
"Hamar yfir mér, helga vé þetta, ok hindra alla illska."

Look down, trace the Kenaz rune while vibrating its name, and say:
"Hamar undir mér, helga vé þetta, ok hindra alla illska."

With arms outstretched, say:
"As Heimdall guards the Bifröst Bridge, may this *vé* be protected from all unholy or unharmonious wights and ways."

Consecrate Altar/Sacred Place

Standing over the table and vibrate the Kenaz rune three times, then say:

"I consecrate this altar and holy place in the name of the gods and goddesses of the folk. May all beings and impure things be banished from this holy place henceforth. As Heimdall guards the Bifröst Bridge, may this *vé* be protected from all unholy or unharmonious wights and ways."

Calling

Standing over the altar or table, call out the following:

"Mighty Thor, red-bearded brother, it is your hammer used in defense of the Gods and Man. Join me here this day as I place a part of my essence in my hammer, to be used as a sign of truth with the Gods of the folk. May all the Gods and Goddesses of my ancestors bear witness to the working here this day. May my ancestors guide me as I sacrifice our essence to bring forth new life. Hail Thor! Hail the Gods and Goddesses! Hail the Ancestors!"

Sacrificing Your Essence

While holding the hammer in your hand, *galdr* the Kenaz rune three times and then say:

"The spark of divinity burns within us all. May a piece of mine be freely given to you to bring forth new life to strengthen the Gods and Man alike."

Take a pin, prick your finger and place a small drop of blood on the *back* of your hammer, as it can damage some materials. *(Note: those in a jail or prison setting can use saliva, which still contains your DNA or essence. This will keep you within the rules and regulations set forth by your institution and not cause any problems.)*

Then say:

"This gift of mine binds us forever. We are one; may you wax and grow in strength and power as you go into darkness for nine nights. May the spark of Divinity within strengthen you as it has strengthened me. May all the Old Ones provide you with what you will need."

Swing the hammer over the candlelight up to the sun or over the picture, saying:

"The light will never let darkness overcome it. Even in dark times, a spark remains, growing and waiting to be reawakened."

As you wrap the hammer into the black or dark cloth, whisper your hammer's name and say: "Sleep now, and grow as a child grows in its mother, awaiting the day of its birth."

Wrap the hammer completely and tie it with twine or thread. Wrap the thread nine times around it, tie it with nine knots, and place it someplace safe. Some of the folk have buried it on their sacred land; others simply put it in a out of the way location.

Part 2

Set up a small altar, table, or property bin with a white cloth or paper marked with runes or symbols on it that mean something to you. I use my rune cloth and lay the wrapped hammer in the center of the altar. Speak while moving to each of the four directions, ending up back in the North as you did in the first part of the ritual.

Hallowing

Trace the Kenaz rune while vibrating its name, and say:
"Hamar í Norðri, helga vé þetta, ok hindra alla illska."

Turn to the East, trace the Kenaz rune while vibrating its name, and say:
"Hamar í Austri, helga vé þetta, ok hindra alla illska."

Turn to the South, trace the Kenaz rune while vibrating its name, and say:
"Hamar í Suðri, helga vé þetta, ok hindra alla illska."

Turn to the West, trace the Kenaz rune while vibrating its name, and say:
"Hamar í Vestri, helga vé þetta, ok hindra alla illska."

Return to the North, look up, trace the Kenaz rune while vibrating its name, and say:

"Hamar yfir mér, helga vé þetta, ok hindra alla illska."

Look down, trace the Kenaz rune while vibrating its name, and say:

"Hamar undir mér, helga vé þetta, ok hindra alla illska."

With arms outstretched, say: "As Heimdall guards the Bifröst Bridge, may this *vé* be protected from all unholy or unharmonious wights and ways."

Consecrate Altar/Sacred Place

Standing in front of the altar or table, *galdr* the Kenaz rune three times, saying:

"I consecrate this altar and holy place in the name of the Gods and Goddesses of the folk. May all beings and impure things be banished from this place or face the hammer of Thor."

Calling

Standing over the table or altar containing the wrapped cloth, say the following:

"I call upon the mighty Thor, welder of Mjölnir, the Gods and Goddesses of old. My ancestral spirits and all beings and wights of the light, come forth and bear witness to the new life which is to come forth this day. Hail Thor! Hail the Gods and Goddesses! Hail the ancestors!"

The Awakening

Standing at the altar, unwrap the twine or thread from the cloth. Open the cloth and whisper your hammer's name into the cloth three times, then say aloud:

"Awaken into the light of day as a child comes forth from its mother's womb! See the happiness you bring to the Gods, to your ancestors, and to me. Come forth and join us now in Midgard."

At this point many people use the twine used in the ritual to hang the hammer around their neck, or transfer it to whatever chain, string, or cord they have planned. Wear your hammer proudly as a sign of your commitment to this way of life.

Closing

Stand in the North and call out:

"I thank the Gods and Goddesses, mighty Thor, my ancestor's spirits and all others for bearing witness to this new life born today. I wish you all well on your journey homeward. Our work here is finished."

Wearing a hammer is something to be proud of, and in many cases it shows you are no longer a young one, but a man or woman on the path, with all rights and responsibilities. You are now expected to act accordingly as a representative of our folk and our way of life.

Hear thou, Loddfáfnir, and heed it well,
Learn it, 'twill land thee strength;
Follow it, 'twill further thee;
If thee list to gain a good woman's love
And all the bliss that be,
Thy troth shall pledge and truly keep:
No one tires of the good he gets.
-The Hávámal

Solitary Blóts

We understand that many individual practitioners have to hold Blót, feast, and sumbel by themselves at times, due to circumstances beyond their control. Here are a few helpful hints: The blóts in this book can be conducted using the same steps and words. You are just going to have to fill all the roles yourself, which really can make it all the more powerful because you only have to worry about remaining focused and having the right intent. If you can do that, you will be fine. As far as ritual tools go, here are some suggestions. Use the back of a writing tablet to make the following:

- Thor's Hammer (You can draw it on paper and sacrifice it afterwards if it's not allowed in your prison or jail, to avoid trouble.)

- Runes

- Galdr

- Sunwheel

- A plastic or paper cup for your horn or bowli (Best if it is used just for ritual purposes; you can put runes or drawings on it that can be easily removed if they are prohibited.)

- A plain sheet of paper marked with meaningful symbols can be your altar cloth (Can be sacrificed after the ritual if you're not allowed to have it.)

- For an altar, I have used my table, my property bin, or my garbage can turned upside down with a towel over it.

- You can have picture of family or friends on the altar to share in the rituals and keep on your mind as you are conducting the Blót.

- For mead, use juice or water.

൪ Take a few moments to clean the area where you are
having the ritual. Your cell is going to become a ritual
area at this time, so show the Gods and your ancestors the
respect them deserve.

Just remember that men and women have faced the same
difficulties you now face, and they found a way to make things work
and honor our Gods and Goddesses, our ancestors, and our future
decendants. We must remember that taking the steps, saying the
words, and having the right intent are the most important things we
can do, even if we have no ritual tools to help us. We are the only tool
the Gods really need, and by finding a way to honor them in word or
deed, we show them our worth and our strength. Stay strong, and
remember no matter what comes your way out of the darkness, the
spark of divinity within will give you all you need to over come.

Fara Með Guðanna!
(Go with the Gods!)

Burial Customs

We felt the need to add this section to simply explain some
funerary customs within our way of life. In a prison environment, we
will probably never have to conduct a funeral; but if asked by the
chaplain or family of one of our kinsfolk, we should have some
answers. Hopefully, this information will give you some ideas.

Our forefathers used almost every possible type of burial practice at
one time or another. Cremation was common, but inhumation
(ordinary burial in the earth) was also practiced. Grave goods could be
very elaborate or very simple. Some graves in the Viking lands
contained a ship or a boat, while others were wooden chamber graves.
Variety was the rule, but we can still discern certain patterns. These
allow us to observe some very ancient traditions which, modified or
not as present-day laws and conditions permit, we can carry into our
own age.

Ritual concern for the dead is shown in the Lay of Sigdrifa; the hero Sigurð is urged to:

Let bath be made
For such men foredone,
Wash thou hands and feet thereof,
Comb their hair and dry them
Ere the coffin has them;
Then bid them sleep full sweetly.

These simple displays of respect for the dead are the first obligations in the burial rite of Ásatrú. Cremation certainly is not mandatory, though our ancestors believed that the flames of the funeral pyre sped the soul of the dead on his or her way to the next world. There is something bright and glorious and purifying about the flames which almost seem to transform the corpse, the clay of inanimate matter, into a radiant being of light.

Grave goods are universal among the burial of pre-Christian Scandinavia. In the case of the wealthy they were extensive and very complete, requiring huge sacrifices and great riches. In other cases, they were meager or even symbolic. The purpose of grave goods was to provide for the needs of the dead during the long journey to the other world, and to establish them in comfort when they arrived. Grave goods are entirely as appropriate today as in the past.

What do grave goods really have to do with the condition or comfort of the dead? Obviously, we can't answer that from direct experience. We do know that they are an integral part of our religious custom which has accumulated a vast store of psychic energy. We must never forget the power of the mind in influencing the plastic process we call reality. Grave goods are used because they are right in a way that transcends the rational. The concept of a journey to be undertaken by the dead gave rise among the ancient Nordics to the custom of Hel shoes. These were tied securely to the feet of the corpse for this arduous trip. This practice can be revived by we who follow Ásatrú today.

Not just any place is suitable for burial. The body or the ashes should be interred on land belonging to the family or clan if at all possible, because the clan member, even if in Valhalla or another abode of the dead, is also considered present in the burial mound looking over the home fields of his kinsmen. Burial in a modern cemetery crammed in tight with a crowd of strangers and cut off from the homeland is a forlorn and lonely alternative, and a disgrace to the society which permits it.

After the burial rites are performed and the grave is filled in, the leveled grave may be surrounded with stones in an oval or boat-shaped configuration. This was common practice during the Viking Age. The idea was that even though it wasn't always possible to give a person a true ship burial, the symbolism was retained in visible and dramatic form. The purpose of the ship, whether symbolic or actual, was to transport the spirit of the dead to their eternal destination. These rocks and the area they dominate acquire a powerful psychic charge capable of influencing those sensitive to their energies. The Viking cemetery at Lindholm Hoje in Denmark has hundreds of these graves, each with its own stone border, and the atmosphere there is intense indeed.

An alternative to this method of grave construction is to build a high mound of dirt over the tomb to serve as a monument to the deceased, and to serve as a residence for a portion of their spiritual entity. A memorial stone or pole can be placed on top of this mound with a suitable runic inscription, perhaps accompanied by one in a modern language.

For those of us serving time, we should at least take the time to raise a horn and share stories about the deceased. In this manner, we are doing our part in keeping their memory alive.

Sacred Lands

Our Sacred Land

by Tyrsoak Josephsson, Author of Our Sacred Land (2003),
Past Goði of Raven Wolf Kindred 1999-2009, and Current
Goði of Guardians of Othala

Ásatrú is a nature religion, and we believe that the land and our unique relationship to it is sacred. We believe that it is necessary to pursue a relationship with the unique land spirits (or "land-wights"), of all places where we practice our religion. Trees, stones, bodies of water, and earthen mounds are known to give refuge to the land spirits, and are also common components of sacred places of Ásatrú worship. It has been this way since the beginning of our people's sacred awareness over eight thousand years ago. It is also imperative to Ásatrú worship that such sacred places be used only by the Ásatrú worshippers, so as not to confuse or do harm to the spirits of the land.

Many religions appear similar on the surface, yet upon reflection, when religions are looked at a bit deeper, one realizes that they are not as compatible as one first thought. Picture, if you will, a group of Southern Baptists being told that they must hold services in a Catholic church. Even with most of the interior changed, the atmosphere in the place would remain a bit uncomfortable for those attending services, and in turn it would cause a loss of focus. Even with the same God (Jesus), their views and ways of doing things are different, and in turn their places of worship are separate.

For those of us who follow the religion of Ásatrú, those same uncomfortable feelings arise when asked to share land with Native American or Wiccan communities. We can highly respect them for holding onto the old ways and honoring their ancestors, but deep down we will all admit to being uncomfortable when using components of a different religion.

Our Gods, Goddesses, ancestral spirits, and land-wights are similar in many ways, yet to each community they are unique, and as such cannot be fully "shared" or connected with by others whose beliefs are different.

We all view nature as being an important part of our religions. When standing upon our sacred land, we can feel the energy of our ancestors and land spirits. That is the connection we are all trying to make. By sharing land and inviting various Gods and Goddesses, land spirits, and our different ancestral spirits, we are creating an environment of confusion. This results in a loss of focus not only for ourselves, but for those spirits that we are calling upon to partake in the Ritual with us.

When I think of the connection our ancestors had to the land and the importance it played in their everyday lives—where harsh elements or bad crops could make life pretty rough for a part of the year—I've come to appreciate the gifts Mother Earth provides. So many today take these gifts for granted. I believe that one of the responsibilities we take upon ourselves in reclaiming land is caring for it in a way where it will be able to provide for those that will come after us. To do this, we must truly bond with the land and sacrifice a part of ourselves to cement this bond.

Land-wights hold a special place in the heart and soul of our people. This is clearly shown in the history of the Landna'ma in Iceland. The immigrants brought with them their ancestral Land-Spirits—the "little ones", or "elves", from their native lands in Scandinavia. We can also look to our ancestors who eventually ended up here in Vinland. Were they any different? I think not. They brought with them the Gods, Goddesses, Land Wights, and Ancestral Spirits as they came to this new world. They resided in the hearts and soul of our ancestors, and they remain with us today, simply waiting to be reawakened.

As we try to once again understand the importance of the land in our lives, let us look to the various sagas and myths to see the way in which our ancestors appreciated just being able to travel and see the world at a time when travel wasn't the easy jaunt that it is today.

Hopefully, one day, many of us will get to travel to some of the sites and places our ancestors lived and held to be sacred. Imagine living fifteen hundred years ago and being truly dependent upon Mother Earth for what you and your families needed to survive. Only when we can understand this mindset will we begin to understand that the history of our ancestors' exploration and trade throughout the world was taken at a time when they needed to find more land and a better climate to grow food in order to survive. Going "a-Viking" wasn't all our ancestors did, regardless of what picture many wish to paint. We have a proud past, and our sagas and our myths provide many exciting tales and lessons to teach our children, including the true importance of life. May we all one day be able to sit upon sacred land around a warm fire and share these same stories that our ancestors shared with their children.

May we also stress the importance of caring for the land when so many others show their disrespect, and do nothing to strengthen their bond with it. Someone has to step up and make a stand. May you look inward and find the strength needed to be that warrior of the Folk today.

May our holy groves once again ring with laughter and cries of joy as our children grow up learning the true meaning of life among nature and all of her wonder.

-Tyrsoak Josephsson

Sacred Places in Ásatrú

Although the history of the Northern People of Europe is in many ways shrouded in the mists of time, one thing we know for certain is that our people have always had an innate sense of the divine. One Mánifestation of the divine has been our reverence of sacred places.

Today we know of many ancient sites which were considered sacred or holy to our ancestors. The great temple at Uppsala in Sweden is one of the best-known from the accounts of Adam of Bremen and Bishop Thietmar of Meresburg. It was a massive and impressive temple where great sacrifices were held to honor Odin, Thór, and Frey. Today, all that remains are the mounds of the great Heathen Kings.

From the Saxons we learn of the great Irminsul, where ceremonies were made to honor Wotan and Donar. The Irminsul was not a temple; it was a sacred place in the forest. The Irminsul itself was thought to be a mighty oak tree. It was a place to sacrifice for victory and prosperity, and is perhaps the most sacred site in continental Europe.

There is no doubt that the thousands of stone monoliths which dot the countryside of Northern Europe were also sacred places. Some of these great stones were erected over ten thousand years ago, and one can still feel the power and energy of these ancient stone sentinels. Some of these stones were set in circles and it is believed that they were the sites of the tribal Things. Such Thing sites have been identified throughout Germany, the British Isles, and the Scandinavian counties. Although the Thing sites may have been governmental in scope, there is no doubt that great Blóts were held there, and the long cherished traditions of the Thing were held to be sacred as well. The greatest of these Thing sites is known as Thingvellir, which is located about seventeen miles east of Reykjavik, Iceland, where the Godar Republic was formed. For seventy years, people lived free of foreign domination and managed their own affairs in harmony with the Gods and Landvættir.

The Sagas also tell us of regional Hofs which were used for Sumbels and feasts. It is believed that the few surviving stave churches in Norway were patterned after the ancient Ásatrú Hofs. Perhaps thousands of these Hofs once dotted the landscape of the North.

It is also known that many natural places were regarded as sacred to the Folk. Mountains, great rock formations, single stones, springs, wells, rivers, and lakes were places of worship, meditation and ceremonies of the Folk. It was common, after great victories of war to cast the booty of the conquered army's weapons into water to give thanks for victory. Certain springs, wells, bogs, and pools of water were repositories of offerings. The ritual of casting runes into a pool of water is still done today with the throwing of coins into a fountain. Everything natural and pure was believed to be home of the land spirits, and they were honored with offerings of food, mead, and ale.

The mounds of the glorious dead were also seen as sacred places, where one could talk to the ancestors in meditation and receive answers to the many questions of life and death.

Although much has changed since ancient times, sacred places remain. Our great groves were desecrated and burned by the pious monks. Our sacred groves were cut down, and the great Irminsul burned, while our Folk were threatened with death if they returned to their sacred places. All the same, our ancient folkways and beliefs prevailed, and we are back to reclaim the sacred and what is rightfully ours. In the few decades since the Founders brought us back our sacred religion, Hofs, grove, and sacred places have been reclaimed by the Folk. Again our people gather in their chosen land to honor and worship the holy Æsir with Blót, Sumbel, and Feast.

In 2236 Runic Era, the first Hof was built for Ásatrú worship in Vinland. On private land in western Arizona, massive oak beams which once were part of a railroad bridge were erected to form the framework of a simple yet impressive building. It was called Odinshof, and was used by the Arizona Kindred for many years. Most recently, the first of what would become an Annual Gathering of the Goðar was held there.

In 2241 Runic Era, the second Ásatrú Hof in Vinland was begun by Robert Taylor and the Tribe of Wulfings. This was the site of the Tyr Blót of Alþing Ten, and since that time it has been used for numerous gatherings of the Wulfing Tribe. It is known as the Vanir Hof; much skill and dedication went into the building of this magnificent example of a sacred temple. To my knowledge, these are the only Hofs built specifically for Ásatrú worship in Midgard in modern times. One would certainly hope that many more will be built by our Kindreds and Tribes in the future.

Today in Vinland, Kindreds choose to worship in groves once again reclaimed for our sacred rites. My Arizona Kindred chose a site in the National Forest which suits our needs perfectly. It is located in an ancient old growth forest of pines, firs, and oaks. A spring-fed brook borders the grounds, which is used for runic workings. Years ago, we performed a land-taking ceremony and buried small rune stones at the cardinal points in the grove. We have used this site for over twenty-five years and we continue to utilize it today. In honor of the great All-Mother, it is known as Frigg's Grove.

I know of several Kindreds who are blessed with large tracts of land and they have erected outdoor altars and built the site specifically for worship. A few hearty souls who enjoy hiking into the mountains to perform their seasonal Blóts at an isolated spring or grove. Others who are unable to travel have a specific site chosen in their yard to perform their Ásatrú rites.

Wherever the site for worship is located, it is important to make contact with the Landvættir, to make your intentions known, and to honor them by protecting the site and keeping it holy. At the ending of each Blót, I use the mead remaining in the bowli as an offering to the Landvættir. It is not just our will and determination which makes a site sacred; it is also the blessing of the Gods and Goddesses in conjunction with the holy spirits of the land itself.

It is our duty as the Ásatrú to protect and defend the unspoiled places left in Midgard. In the future our children and following generations of the Ásatrú will find these places to call their own and make them sacred as well. It is important to protect our ancient sites from future desecration and vandalism by governments and land developers.

Valgard Murray, Allsherjargodi, Ásatrú Alliance
Director, World Tree Outreach Ministry
Horning 2253 Runic Era

He knows alone who has wandered wide,
and far has fared on the way,
what manner of mind a man doth own
who is wise of head and heart.
The Hávámal

The Meaning of a Sacred Place

At the time of his death in October of 1987, Joseph Campbell was the world's foremost authority on mythology. A preeminent scholar, writer and teacher at Sarah Lawrence College for almost forty years, he was once asked, "What does it mean to have a sacred place?"

He replied, "This is an absolute necessity for anyone today. This is a place where you can simply experience and bring forth what you are and what you might be. This is the place of creative incubation. At first you may find that nothing happens there, but if you have a sacred place and use it, something eventually will happen."

People claim the land by creating sacred sites. By mythologizing the animals and plants, they invest the land with spiritual power. It becomes a temple and a place for meditation. One should find the symbol in the landscape itself of the energies of the life there. This is what all early traditions do. They sanctify their own landscapes.

—"Joseph Campbell and the Power of Myth"
Public Affairs Television

L'anse aux Meadows

In the early sixties, Norwegian explorer Helge Ingstad and his wife, archaeologist Anne Stine Ingstad, went to Newfoundland to explore a place identified on an Icelandic map from the 1670s as *Promontorium Winlandiar* near a small fishing village of L'Anse aux Meadows. They believed that it might mark the location of an ancient Norse settlement.

Finding it turned out to be easier than they could have imagined. When they asked the locals if there were any odd ruins in the area, they were immediately taken to a place known as "the Indian Camp". They immediately recognized the grass-covered ridges as Viking-era ruins like those in Iceland and Greenland.

During the next seven years, the Ingstads and an international team of archaeologists exposed the foundation of eight separate buildings, sitting on a terrace between two bogs. They also found a "Celtic"-style bronze pin with a ring-shaped head similar to ones the Norse used to fasten their cloaks, a bone needle and a small whetstone for sharpening scissors and needles.

Further excavation in the mid-seventies led some to believe this was likely the place that Leif Eriksson camped in his discovery of Vinland. Scraps of wood were subsequently radio carbon dated to somewhere between 980 and 1020, which is when Leif was to have visited Vinland. Some archaeologists have figured this site was home to about five hundred people. How long they stayed there or what type of life they lived we cannot say, only that this is probably the first time our ancestors set foot on North America.

The Vix Grave

In an upper valley of the Seine, a woman's body, adorned with ornate jewelry, was discovered sitting in a wagon in the center of a burial mound. Various items were found including bowls, jugs, and other vessels. One huge vessel had various scenes depicted upon it, including a scene showing a woman who appeared to be a Seeress with an outstretched arm. It was thought that this huge ornate vessel could have been used for sacrifices, as it was considered too large for the usual uses. This burial, and the way the mound was arranged, would suggest that this woman was special; she could have been a priestess of a local temple or perhaps a Seeress herself. At this time, due to lack of literature left behind about burials during this time period, we might never know the true story of the woman in the Vix grave.

The Memorial Stones of Gotland

Gotland is a small island in the Baltic. It was an important stop for those traveling from Sweden to the countries in Eastern Europe. Over time, the island and those living there became quite wealthy with all the travelers stopping off. While it is small, it is dotted with what could be called memorial stones. The pictures show traces of color, and most of them have ships and spiral designs on them. Some are even designed with various scenes which may possibly reflect the beliefs that our ancestors had about the afterlife. Many of these had a scene which showed a warrior on a horse being greeted by a woman holding up a horn. Some say this relates to warriors being welcomed to Valhalla, as this scene is often depicted on the top of the stone. Others show a ship with a horse riding above it. Could these be the Valkyries we read of in our mythology and Sagas? A few scenes also show a rider on an eight-legged steed. Could this be the mighty Odin riding Sleipnir across the skies? Odin was one of the Gods our ancestors held in high regard. No wonder, then, that he would be remembered by our ancestors as they created these stones that are truly works of art.

Ships are also depicted on numerous stones. Our ancestors traveled the seas in ships on trade missions, in search of other lands, and when they went "a-Viking", so the ship played an important part in their lives. The ship is also viewed as the vehicle that carries the dead to other lands, and many grave sites are marked with stones in the shape of a ship. There is also evidence of burials taking place in ships—in some cases the ships were buried in bogs, sunk in the seas, or simply buried in the earth.

The reason these stones were put up might never be known. It could have been a memorial to a loved one who died or never returned, or a way of honoring someone. Whatever the case may be, we can be thankful to the ones who had them created. They gave us a look at some of the things important to our ancestors at this time in history.

Aulnay-aux-Planches

Located in France, Aulnay-aux-Planches consists of three cemeteries which are all a bit different, yet they all seem connected as a group. The first shows flat cremation-type graves. The second seems to be marked or protected by stones with a large ritual area nearby, although we cannot be certain of the rituals performed there. The third area contains some graves which are surrounded by stones.

We are unsure of the meaning of the separation among these graves. From the various animal bones present, it is presumed that some sort of animal sacrifices were conducted. The sacrifices may have been within the context of rituals that took place at funerals or perhaps a feast held in honor of certain Deities. The identities of the grave occupants and the various alignments of stones are unclear, yet it is clear that this was truly a special place at one time to our ancestors even if the meaning has been obscured by the passage of time.

A site at Helgo in Sweden yielded twenty-six brooches which show a man facing a woman separated by a leaf or branch. This site is thought to be a sacred place that was used for gatherings and feasts held in honor of the Vanir, deities associated with farmers in the community who were seeking blessings upon their land and themselves. Another group of brooches was found hidden in holes which were thought to support posts in an old temple which was buried under a Christian church. We don't know why these special brooches were placed there; perhaps they were put there by someone holding onto the old ways as a new religion took over in their community. But we can be sure that they were put there for a reason, and perhaps one day the answer will be brought to light.

Temple in Uppsala, Sweden

One of the last great temples sacred to our Gods was destroyed in the year 1100 C.E. by Christian missionaries attempting to kill off heathen beliefs. They destroyed the temple, but the way of life our ancestors lived continues to this day. This same sacred temple was where the first Reawakening is said to have started, and it will forever remain a special place where our Gods and Goddesses once roamed.

Gravesites of Bjorko

On the small island of Bjorko ("Birka") is one of Sweden's oldest towns. Founded somewhere around 800 C.E., in its prime Bjorko was a great center of trade, a large market town with several harbors for the numerous ships that would stop here. A huge fort guarded the town and its people. There are over three thousand graves there, many still surrounded by a pattern of stones which is now considered a typical Viking grave, representing a symbolic death ship to carry warriors who had died fighting to Valhalla.

Many of these graves were found to contain treasures from around the world. It would seem that the locals were cremated and buried outside of town, since the mounded graves contained mostly Scandinavian goods. The merchants, on the other hand, were given unburned burials inside the town, and these graves yield treasures from abroad. The Viking graves, marked with the pattern of a ship, again show the importance our ancestors placed upon lending permanency to a special place. Being able to create a ritual site similar to these would certainly put us into an environment where we would feel connected to our ancestors and the way of life they once lived.

In *A History of the Vikings*, Gwyn Jones writes: "In the grave illustrated (Birka 581), a fighting man has been laid to rest with everything he could require in the next world: two shields (one at his feet, one above his head), axe, sword, dagger, knife, two dozen arrows (we presume with a wooden bow), two spears, stirrups, and two horses, as well as a comb and bowl and other objects. A silver *dirhem* found under the skeleton, which must have been minted 913-33, allows us to date the interment in the period 913-c. 980."

The Centre of Yeavering

A high rounded hill above the river Derwent yielded evidence of two halls; one was thought to be a temple or a place of assembly where the people gathered to offer sacrifice. Evidence was also found of an outdoor wooden amphitheater where people could gather, said to be lare enough to hold a great number of people. This was one of only a few sites that show the possibility (due to the presence of animal bones) of people gathering for religious feasts and sacrifices. The name of a nearby town was Gefrin, meaning Hill of Goats, and a goat skull was found in one man's grave there and a single ox tooth in another. The meaning is unclear, but it certainly had some importance at the time of these burials.

Frequently Asked Questions about "Our Sacred Land"

When is a place considered sacred to the Ásatrú?

The Ásatrú believe that a place becomes sacred when something special is seen or felt to have happened there. Certain people feel connected to that event or "Happening" at that site.

What type of event or "something special happening" are you talking about?

It may be a historical event, or something on a more personal level, such as someone making a connection to the Gods, Disir, or Landvættir during a ritual. Once this connection has happened, then something truly special has occurred. The Raven Wolf Kindred has had an occasion where two ravens landed and watched a ritual being performed. A few brothers have seen our ritual circle surrounded by warriors of old watching as we held our Blót/Feast/Sumbel. These are truly special occasions that have strengthened our belief in the importance of having our own sacred land and the opportunity to honor our ancestors there.

Do other religions have sacred sites?

It would be safe to say that most religions today have various places throughout the world that they consider sacred to them. There are various holy sites in the world considered sacred to the Christian, Islamic, or Jewish faiths. Other examples are the huge statues of Buddha throughout Asia, the sacred sites of the Hindus, and the sacred lands of the Native Americans. There are various temples, churches, burial grounds, and similar sites throughout Egypt, South America, Easter Island and Stonehenge. We could go on and on, but rather, let us simply say that we realize that all of these places are truly unique and special for various religions and should be treated with respect by all.

Can't these sites be sacred to all people?

These are all places with which certain peoples feel a connection. That is why, throughout history, they have been sacred to those certain people. Many others with different beliefs can visit them, and many say they can feel an energy or presence in these special places. but without a personal connection to that place, all that results is a special feeling beneath which the deeper meaning cannot be grasped.

These sites throughout the world are certainly very special. Those people with a connection to them should attempt to visit them within their lifetimes and discover the importance and meaning of them to themselves, taking the time to pay honor and respect to their Ancestors in their own special way. That is what makes each group of people unique.

Why can't a place sacred to the Ásatrú be used by people of other religions?

Each religion has similar beliefs, yet each is unique in their own way. It is that uniqueness that makes those people special. In Ásatrú, we use rituals to make a connection to our Gods and Goddesses, our land-wights and our Ancestral Spirits. This connection and bond strengthens both ourselves and the entity that we make a connection to. Many of us have found a new strength and direction after such an experience. For those followers of our religion seeking such an experience, being in an environment that is comfortable allows us to focus on the meaning of the ritual without any disruptions which could cause a loss of focus. A space filled with various spirits or the energy of other religions or people would cause a distraction and loss of focus. For many of us, this would cause the ritual to be disrupted, useless, and perhaps even harmful.

Once a place is considered sacred, is there something special you need to do?

There are numerous things you can do. One is to always have an Oath Ring present during rituals. In the days of our Ancestors, the very presence of an Oath Ring was said to make a place sacred. There are also land-taking rituals which bond the land to the people performing the ritual. We feel that with each ritual or gathering of the clan at the sacred site, the presence of energy grows stronger and the bond between the land-wights and the people gathered there becomes even stronger.

Once a bond is initially made by a certain group of people, some sort of ritual should be performed where you would sacrifice to the land-wights and let them know your intentions. (We've included a land-taking ritual in this book.) Once this ritual is performed, a bond is forged, and the people and the land become connected to each other. Anyone else then trying to use the land for another purpose would then be considered to be intruding by the people connected to the sacred land and the spirits gathered there.

How often do you use your sacred site?

At least once a month we hold a gathering where we perform Blót/Feast/Sumbel, and then Rune Guild or Warriors Guild holds all their rituals there. At least a couple of times a year, we also perform a ritual to the land-spirits and the Fire Hearth.

Sometimes we will simply gather around a fire and share stories, as our Ancestors did. We feel that any time the clan gathers and the opportunity allows, we should gather at our sacred site. In the winter months it seems to be less often, but whenever we perform rituals or in times of deep thinking on the mysteries of life, we would use our sacred land. It is here that a connection to our Gods and Goddesses and the land spirits would be stronger than in a chapel used by others. The environment of our sacred land comforts us in a way where we feel at ease, as if we were in our mother's arms.

Do we need a sacred outdoor site to practice Ásatrú?

Ásatrú, the indigenous religion of the Northern European peoples, is a nature-based practice in which the followers celebrate their closeness to the Gods and Goddesses of the Folk—as well as the tribal ancestors and land spirits—by closely communing with nature. Our ancestors did not enclose faith within cold walls; rather, they would sing their praise to the open skies, likewise we do the same. From ancient times they have gathered in the sacred groves and upon holy high places to open themselves up to the unalterable laws of nature. To force the faithful to hide their ways within a cold, stark room, unable to sense the presence of their Mother the Earth or their Sky Father, is a crime not only against the true Folk, but also against nature itself. When the religious bond with nature is severed, a part of the true Folk soul will die.

How can I get a kindred started and get an outdoor area approved for our use?

For those of you who have begun to feel the pull of your ancestral memories, a good place to start is to continue to read all you can on the religion and way of life called Ásatrú. Then meet with other like-minded individuals and share what you have learned. This book contains all the information you need to get started, whether you are in the free-world or in a prison. To start a kindred or create your own sacred space, read through the examples of kindred organization in the appendixes and discuss them with others who will be part of the kindred. Take your time, and make any decisions after much thought and discussion to avoid any problems from coming up later.

Construction of a Ritual Area

Description and Dimensions

Circle of Mystery. This is a 26-foot-diameter circle marked with stones. It is within this circle that the faithful gather to commune with their Gods, Goddesses, and nature during religious rites. The circle should measure 26 feet in diameter with a rise from 0″ at the outside to 6-8″ at the center. This requires 5¾ ton of dirt to be compacted.

Ancestral Meditation Path. The path should be a 1½-foot-wide circular path which surrounds the Circle of Mystery. This requires two tons of pea-gravel in a path with the sod removed.

Fire of Ancestral Oath. The fire pit is placed in the center of the circle of mystery. The fire is a living entity which represents the unity of the family and Kindred in their daily fight against the darkness which seeks to capture man's soul. The fire is also a divinatory and sacrificial tool. The fire pit should measure three feet in diameter by one and a half to two feet deep. The top edge is circled with stones 6″ to 8″ in size. You will need one bale of straw to mix with dampened dirt removed from the pit to plaster stones to the pit wall. These stones are 2″- 3″, and you will need approximately 200 lbs. The fire must be built to bake stones in fire-pit wall. The total circle diameter is 29″.

Ritual Altar, or *Stalli.* This is the consecrated platform upon which sacred relics and tools are placed during ritual. The altar should measure 4′ x 2′, with a top of concrete or oak. Runes should be carved on each side of the top, with legs on each side made of laid stone or brick on an 18″ x 2′ x 16″ deep footing of concrete per side. This altar sits at the (first) North inside area of the Circle of Mystery, facing South.

Longship of Ancestral Way. This is comprised of stones, placed in the shape of a long-ship. This ship outline is a representation of our ancestral burial mounds. When faced with the great questions of life, just as our ancestors before us, we sit upon the burial mounds of those who have gone before to communicate with them. We seek the lore that is gained by making the journey in a spiritual sense, hoping to be reborn with a greater understanding of the mysteries of life. The longship should measure 13′ x 4′ with pointed bow ends.

A four-foot mast-pole should be in the center with a broken and burnt top. The mast pole, as in history, is a place to hang the kindred banner when making a spiritual journey. As you approach the distant realms, it allows those who dwell there to know the one who was brave enough to make the journey, and to welcome them properly.

The mast-pole is circled with stones, with burnt log embers placed within the circle of stones. Sod in the shape of a ship is removed, with stones—24 in all, 6"-8"—placed in the area where the sod is removed to create a runic circle for ancestral travel to Valhalla. This ship stands 10' from the Circle of Mystery to the West.

Juniper Bushes. Two are required; one stands on each side of the altar. The Juniper tree represents Yggdrasill (the World Tree), which is the central axis of the universe around which the Nine Worlds are arrayed. The tree also represents the human nervous system, along which our life force travels. The reason for two trees is symbolically taken from myth as man and woman were created from two trees (Ash and Elm) by the Gods.

Ritual Tool Storage Box. This is a storage cabinet for ritual items that are to be used in the holy rites of Ásatrú. This cabinet should be able to be secured in some way. Built by Mechanical Services, the ritual tool storage box should measure 4' wide x 8' long x 4' deep and 3/4" or 5/8" thick. Box should have two shelves and two doors in front with a rubber door-seal and locking capacity.

Woodpile Shelter This is a 2' x 6' area consisting of four poles with an overhanging roof for the orderly storage of firewood to be used during rituals. Alternately, one could have a **Wood Storage Box.** Built by mechanical services, the wood storage box should be a size similar to ritual tool box.

Split Rail Fence. A fence with gate serves the purpose of separating holy ground from that which is mundane. The fence is a boundary marker, but it is not intended to keep one in or out. The boundary fence may be as simple as split rail or rope and post, or as complex as you like it. This area will be 50 feet by 50 feet. We prefer a double-rail 4-sided fence, with the open gate at South and the top bar 4' from ground, and 3" wide. Measurements are 55' x 55'. 12 L-hooks should be attached on the inside of the fence to hang Warrior Shields.

Banner Poles. The kindred banner serves the dual purpose of strengthening the ancestral bond and informing those who approach the kindred holding just who the Kindred is, so that ritual and very formalized greetings may be exchanged. Four 6' x 4" poles should be anchored in the ground to support the kindred banner.

Water Source. A well or pump should be close by in order to acquire water for rituals. Ideally, the circle should be near a sacred spring or well, but this is not always possible.

Land Claiming Ritual

Our ancestors have always had a unique relationship with the land and the spirits that dwell upon it. During rituals, a sacrifice was offered up to the land and to the Alfar and Disir. These gifts were freely given, and a gift was given in return, which was a bond between our ancestors and the spirits of the land where they held their sacred rituals. Once this bond was made, it was an obligation of the Folk to care for and protect the land. At times our ancestors gave their lives while protecting their sacred groves. In today's world, we are expected to do the same. We find our "sacred land" and we perform a ritual where we begin bonding with the land. We mark the area we consider sacred with either a physical marker, or we can walk the boundary of the land we wish to "connect with".

This ritual greets the Alfar and the Disir, the spirits of the land that we are seeking to bond with. We offer gifts to strengthen those that dwell there; by doing this, we are making an outward sign that we wish to bond with them. Then we must look inward and allow this bond to grow strong. The following is an idea for a ritual for bonding with your land.

(Note: You might wish to have a fire burning beforehand, or at least have a torch or candle on hand. You will also need some mead or some other liquid to fill the Horn.)

The Godi or Gydja performs the Hammer sign to the four cardinal directions, and then moves to the center of the land with others that have assembled there. They call out in a loud voice:

"Hail to you, Alfar and mighty Disir and all creatures that dwell in this place. We come here to honor our Gods and Goddesses in the old ways, as our ancestors did before us. We come to offer sacrifice and forge a bond with you that can never be broken. Hail to us, and hear our words."

The Godi or Gydja raises the Horn filled with mead or other liquid, and calls out:

"I bid you welcome. I offer sacrifice as in days of old. May this sacrifice, freely given, strengthen you in your time of need." (Pour some mead onto the ground.)

The Horn is then passed to the next person, who speaks words similar to those above. Each person's heart will bring out what this occasion means to them, and that is what you are seeking to do. The spirits of the land will be watching your actions and listening to your words, so it is best if they truly come from your heart.

The Godi or Gydja then takes up the torch or candle, and calls out:

"May this fire, which has warmed our ancestors' homes, cooked their food, and burned their dead, be a sign of that eternal flame within. At times it might burn dim, but it can never be extinguished. May it burn bright now for all to see as we walk our sacred land, to awaken and welcome all that dwell here. Holy ones that dwell here, this sacred place is your home. We honor you and this holy place as our own. May we all grow stronger for the betterment of the Folk. Hail to you!"

Once everyone is done, the Godi or Gydja closes the ritual. You should then have a large feast where cries of joy will once again be heard in a now sacred place. Use your land often, and honor the commitment you have made to it.

Appendixes

Appendix I: Proposal for Starting a Kindred

From "Our Sacred Land" by Tyrsoak Josephsson

What follows is a proposal/plan/request by the Ásatrú practitioners in this prison for the opportunity to establish an Ásatrú community and acquire an outside ritual area for our community to practice our religious way of life with some semblance of historic tradition. We have attempted to provide a detailed explanation of the elements needed to make our community and ritual area a working reality within the Ásatrú way of life. A great deal of reference material has been listed to show the validity of this request, as well as points of contact both within and outside the Federal Bureau of Prisons.

Ásatrú is a sincere religious group striving for spiritual recollection with their ancestral heritage. We are asking for nothing more than what is ours by right as per the U.S. Constitution, the Director of Chaplain's services in Washington D.C., and the Office of the Regional Chaplain.

Thank you for your time in this matter.

Hail the Gods and Goddesses!

Long before Christianity came to northern Europe, the people there had their own way of life and religion. One of the more widespread was Ásatrú, practiced in the lands that are today the Scandinavian countries, the Netherlands, Germany, France, Austria, Switzerland, Ireland, the Baltic States, northern Russia, and other dominions. Ásatrú is the native religion of those aforementioned areas.

We believe in an underlying spiritual presence that exists within all living things in the form of all-pervading energy—plants, animals, humans, etc.—in fact, in all matter coexistent with nature. We further believe that this spiritual energy, or reality, is interdependent with us. In other words, we affect it and it affects us. We are likewise aware of a diverse group of deities—Oþinn, Baldr, Thor, Freyja, and many others—who we believe we are descended from, and who we have contact with in the forms of Gods and Goddesses of our ancient Northern European heritage.

These divine beings sometimes make themselves known to us in traditional and/or nontraditional forms, oftentimes within the realm of naturally occurring events. Stories about these deities within our Sagas and Eddas are a mysterious language through which these divine beings speak to us. We believe in standards of behavior which are consistent with these spiritual truths, and harmonious with our deepest being. Qualities we hold in high regard are strength, courage, joy, honor, freedom, loyalty to kin, realism, vigor, and honoring our ancestors. To express these factors in our lives is virtuous, and this we strive to perfect and apply.

Here at (name of prison), we wish to form a kindred in belief and way of life with our Gods, Ancestors and compliance in respect of nature or the natural way of life. A kindred is, in reality, an extended family and is usually made up of related and nonrelated individuals. However, unlike most other religious groups and organizations, the relationships between members of a kindred is more like a close-knit tribe where everyone is a blood relative. These are not just idle words or boast. As it says in the "Song of Folk", "Let every enemy beware, when the kinfolk call, we shall be there ... in tribal pride and passion deep, eternal honor we shall keep."

The Way of the Kindred

As mentioned above, within the framework of the kindred, all are equal; all are freemen or freewomen. With this equality comes rights and obligations that are not taken lightly. We are a functional family (as opposed to dysfunctional); all are brothers and sisters. If a member of the kindred experiences a problem in their life that he or she cannot deal with alone, they have the right (and obligation) to meet with the kindred to seek help in resolution of the problem. The kindred, as a group, then takes on the role of parent, advisor, guardian, etc., doing whatever is within their powers to resolve the problem.

Of course, the individual has the obligation to live their life in an honorable and responsible manner. They should not see the kindred as a way out of situations brought about by indiscretions on their part. In other words, the kindred should not be looked upon as a fix-all for an individual's neglect of responsibility. However, except in the case of dishonor, the kindred is not there to pass judgment on its members, and will be there for them when the need arises.

It is the responsibility of all kindred members to honor and respect the rights of all other members. When a dispute arises between members of the kindred, the kindred (or an appointed committee of kindred members) *on request only* will meet to discuss, attempt to resolve, and—if need be—vote on a particular situation. Members are expected to abide by the kindred decision. Failure to do so may result in an individual being ousted from the kindred. Reentry into the kindred is possible with resolution of the problem.

Individual members are expected to act in an honorable manner when in the public eye, in keeping with the values of Ásatrú. Bringing dishonor onto the kindred or Ásatrú itself may be cause for expulsion from the kindred.

Individual members have the right and obligation to attend as many of the holy Blóts and Sumbels as they are able. An individual may, of course, leave the kindred at any time for whatever reason. Ásatrú is not a cult religion, and we love our freedom too much to ever hand it over to someone else.

Our ancient Ancestors were brave and bold souls, and the modern Ásatrú kindred reflects this. We are a tight-knit tribe! As the saying goes, "The strength of the Wolf is the pack, the strength of the pack is the Wolf." So it is with the kindred.

In order to perform rituals and allow the kindred to assemble for fellowship and learning the ways of our religion, a purified ground must be maintained. The area needed for the assembly of the kindred must be unblemished by others. We fully acknowledge the fact that security must be maintained in that area. An explanation and diagram is covered in the section labeled "Land Proposal".

Appendix II:
Membership in Guardians of Othala Kindred

(This, and the document on Kindred Structure that follows, have been included in the book as an example of how to organize membership requirements in a kindred. Feel free to take inspiration from us, or create your own membership rules.)

Membership in the Guardians of Othala kindred is open to anyone of Northern European ancestry who are interested in learning about the Northern Tradition and honoring their ancestors in word and deed. The Guardians of Othala is a folkish Odinist kindred registered with the Ásatrú Alliance. We practice Odinism, but acknowledge some of the heroes and ways of our members.

Our kindred is completely self-supporting through donations from its members and well-wishers who want to help further our cause. All potential members need to be familiar with the Runes, Sagas, and Eddas. We make no excuses or apologies for our beliefs. We practice a strict code of honor and discipline which we expect our members to follow. Any member who does not, or who brings dishonor to the kindred, will be brought before members of the High Seat who will judge them according to our laws. A sentence of outlawry can be imposed, at which time the member will be immediately expelled.

Each membership application will be reviewed and checked for dishonorable crimes and actions, especially against children, women and the elderly. Membership will be decided on a case-by-case basis.

The Guardians of Othala Kindred has three levels of membership to allow you, the individual, to get to know the kindred structure and its members before making a formal commitment and becoming a sworn member.

Associate Member

Associate Membership is offered to men and women (free or incarcerated) who are practicing the Northern or Celtic Tradition, or have family members who are doing so. Associate Members may request a Rune casting and/or counseling from a member of the kindred High Seat or their delegates.

Incarcerated Associate Members may request to purchase books (new or used) at cost plus shipping. The kindred cannot be held responsible if your correctional institution denies the publication.

Provisional Member

Provisional Members are those individuals who are interested in one day becoming Full Members with all rights and responsibilities. They are expected to take a more active role in the business of the kindred. In doing so, they will show Full Members the part they might one day fill in the web that binds us all together.

Provisional Members *must* ask a Full Member to foster them. This member will be responsible for guiding this "new one" down the path as they seek to educate themselves in the Old Ways. In many cases, a Provisional Member will take part of the name of the the one guiding them as a sign of respect. (i.e. Joseph: Josephsson or Josephsdottir)

Provisional Members are expected to acquire a basic understanding of the Old Ways by educating themselves to the standards set by the kindred High Seat, which includes the Runes, Gods/Goddesses, rituals, the Nine Worlds and their wights, importance of Blót, Feast and Sumbel, the Sacrifices of Odin, the Hávamal, and the importance of our myths. They are expected to be able to conduct a Blót, Feast, and Sumbel prior to becoming a Full Member, and are expected to handle themselves in a manner that will bring honor upon themselves, the kindred and The Folk.

Provisional Members may be put forth for Full Membership by their fosterer when they feel they are ready to acquire all rights and responsibilities of a Full Member. Members must take the Oath To The Kindred before a Full Member. If not possible due to physical restrictions, a High Seat may assist the member in performing the Oath before the Gods.

Full Member

Full Members have all the rights of an Associate and Provisional Member, as well as the right to preside over a Blót, Feast or Sumbel. They have the right to vote on all matters put forth to a kindred vote.

Full Members have the right to foster someone if they so choose, and the right to petition for a position on the High Seat, or other ranking positions (ie. Lord/Lady, Skald, Keeper of the Ritual Items). They have the right to invite guests to kindred functions, as well as the right, after being given the blessing of the High Seat.

Full Members wishing to become a member of the HighSeat must show that they have published a work based upon their beliefs in the Northern Tradition (Odinism, Ásatrú, Celtic Tradition) in a recognized publication. This is to show us that you are willing to put forth effort to educate others about our faith and keep it alive.

Full Members must have an advanced education in the Runes, Nine Worlds and the Gods/Goddesses. Rune work is essential. Every Full Member must strive to unlock the secrets of each rune. They must attempt to utilize the runes to traverse all Nine Worlds. They must also be able to dissect the Havamal and The Lay of Rig.

Full Members are the forward-facing representatives of our kindred. It is their responsibility to uphold our principles and the spirit of Othala.

Let no man glory in the greatness of his mind,
but rather keep watch o'er his wits.
Cautious and silent let him enter a dwelling;
to the heedful comes seldom harm,
for none can find a more faithful friend
than the wealth of mother wit.
-The Hávámal

Appendix III: Kindred Structure

The Ásatrú Kindred

The Ásatrú/Odinist kindred constitutes an extended family of sorts, whereby those new to our ancestral ways may be instructed in the proper application of their religion in daily life.

This nation has always recognized the sanctity of every religious tradition. Regardless of its origin, the notion, therefore, that solitary practice of Ásatrú is sufficient to satisfy the needs of our religious practice does not bear the same concern for those of European descent as is shown for those of Middle Eastern, American Indian, Jewish, or African descent. Such a notion ignores the spiritual needs of those who have embraced the ancient religious tradition of our European ancestors. To those of us with this heritage, the kindred structure is of paramount importance, providing three progressive avenues of inner development:

- It provides a link to our religious archetypes, and allows for the development of our religious consciousness.
- It serves as a vehicle of expression for that which we learn, and for our acquired consciousness of duty and honor.
- It facilitates awareness of the negative thoughts and often confused feelings of alienation which plague many of our youth today. It provides constructive methods for dealing with those thoughts and feelings.

In Ásatrú, we have no absolute religious dogma which everyone is required to follow, so kindred structures may vary in certain respects. We do, nevertheless, have guidelines which are based on ancient tradition, and therefore maintain a a Chieftain and a Goði at the head of each kindred. In addition, two or more of the following should be either selected or elected: A Lawspeaker, a Skald, a Secretary, a Librarian, an "Erulian" or Rune Master, and a Rune Instructor.

A **Chieftain's** primary responsibility is to ensure health and well-being of the kindred and it's members. His/Her secondary responsibility is to oversee kindred business as it relates to membership, public relations, government/administrative staff, and legal matters. A **Goði/Gyðja** is the kindred Holy person. His/Her primary responsibility is to ensure the spiritual health of the kindred and its members. He/She will lead the blót, feast and Sumbel, teach members about the Gods/Goddesses, Runes, lore, Eddas, Sagas, and perform the burial/cremation rites for members and their families. A **Drighten's** primary responsibility are to ensure the physical safety of kindred members and to uphold kindred law. In the times of our ancestors, the Drighten would lead war parties to conquer and plunder in the name of the Chieftain and the kindred. A **Lawspeaker's** primary responsibility is to work with the Chieftain to establish kindred bylaws and make them known to the kindred members. He/She represents the kindred in any legal matters when necessary. A **Skald** is responsible for keeping records of the kindred (or extended family tree, so to speak), as well as any noteworthy Sagas. The Skald may also compose poetry if he is so disposed. Some kindreds feel the need for a **Secretary** who is responsible for keeping the minutes of each meeting as well as facilitating interaction between kindred members and the Chaplain. The Secretary also keeps track of legal developments, oaths, and both financial and project-oriented responsibilities. A **Librarian** is responsible, of course, for keeping a record of all kindred books, and making sure that they are returned to the locker by those who have checked them out. An **Erulian** can serve the kindred by protecting the group against unwanted influences from other realms. In addition, the kindred can turn to the Erulian in times of need for divinatory guidance in any matter whatsoever. A **Rune Instructor**, of course, is given the responsibility, of teaching a rune class for those who wish to further their own knowledge.

In a properly structured kindred, those with knowledge will find a vehicle for expanding that knowledge, and the newcomers will find the foundation they need for establishing themselves on the spiritual path of their ancestors. In addition, many of our youth today have difficulty in relating to moral standards from the perspective of obedience to authority. A properly structured kindred, however, can assist them in relating to moral standards from the perspective of duty and honor, and thereby foster a sense of purpose and virtue among our Folk once again.

It is most certainly imperative that we have kindred organizations for the practice of the Ásatrú religion, particularly in the prison setting. May we all seek spiritual attunement to our ancestral Gods and Goddesses through the guidance and support of our kindreds in Ásatrú.

> *I counsel thee, Stray-Singer, accept my counsels,*
> *they will be thy boon if thou obey'st them,*
> *they will work thy weal if thou win'st them:*
> *growl not at guests, nor drive them from the gate*
> *but show thyself gentle to the poor.*
> *Mighty is the bar to be moved away*
> *for the entering in of all.*
> *Shower thy wealth, or men shall wish thee*
> *every ill in thy limbs.*
> *-The Hávámal*

Appendix IV: Our Kindred Oath

I_____ freely swear this oath before the gathered folk, the Gods and Goddesses, my ancestors and all beings throughout the Nine worlds and my future descendants whom I strive for in deed and word.

I swear to my sworn brothers and sisters in the Guardians of Othala that as long as I breathe I will bow to no man and yield only to the Gods. I will seek out the mysteries of the ancient ways of my ancestors as I walk the path the Norns have placed before me. I will strive daily to bring glory and honor to my kindred and clan.

I will live by the nine noble virtues, the six fold goal and all the other honorable creeds that show me how to be an honorable man/woman striving to make the future a better one for my race, kindred, my clan and future descendants.

To my sworn-brothers and sisters I give my loyalty and sword to the kindred. I will not flee from any man who is my equal in bravery and arms. I will bow to no man in victory or defeat, and will yield only to Gods. I will avenge any of my oath-bound brothers threefold as though we are brothers and sisters by blood.

I will not utter words of fear or ever give up no matter how hard things appear. I will uphold the beliefs and traditions of my ancestors and will be held accountable for my actions. I will stand beside my kindred through thick and thin, good and bad.

I will do right by my kindred and do what I can to help my brothers and sisters and do it to the best of my ability. I will promote our kindred's mission so that others will know they are not forgotten behind prison walls.

If I break this oath, I betray my kindred and my Folk and I acknowledge that I have betrayed my ancestors and my future descendants. I will be known to all as an oathbreaker. Let me know no peace or find no succor in all my travels. All doors once open to me will now be barred.

Appendix V: Old Norse Pronunciation

a   as in artistic

á   as in father

e   as in men

é   as in bay "ay"

i   as in it

í   as ee in feet

o   as in omit

ó   as in ore

ø, ö   as in not

u   as in put

ú   as in rule

æ   as ai as in hair

œ   as u in slur

y   as u in German Hütte (i)

ý   as u in German Tür (ee)

au   as ou in house

ei, ey as ay in May

j   as in year

rl   as dl

rn   as dn

nn   as dn after long vowels

H   is silent if it is the first letter of a word followed by a consonant (i.e. Hlín would be pronounced Lín)

Þ, þ   as th in "they" (called "thorn")

Ð, ð   as th in "with" (called "eth")

Appendix VI: Dietary Standards

There are several foods that are sacred to the Gods and Goddesses of Ásatrú and to those of us who follow this way of life. I will explain what some of these foods are and why we hold them sacred, and also where you can find more important information on them if need be.

ଔ **PORK:** Pork is one of the most sacred of the foods to Ásatrú and this way of life. In the Lay of Grímnir (Grímnismál) we are told that in Valhalla the divine Boar Saehrimnir is slaughtered daily for the chosen of the slain to feast upon and gain strength for the next day's battles. From this alone, we can see that pork is a very sacred food to our way of life. Pork is also the main food for the Frey feast for our people and their way of life. There are references to pork in many other lays, and in the book *Myths of the Norsemen,* pp. 19-22.

ଔ **OXEN:** Oxen or bull is the meat of the Gods and Kings. In the lays, myths, and sagas, we learn that the biggest and best oxen and bulls (usually black ones) were held above other meats for only the most special feasts. They were usually eaten on special occasions such as dining with a God, a feast for a King, or very valiant and mighty warriors. The feasts of oxen are told of numerous times in the Lays such as the *Lay of Thrym* (23), and the *Lay of Hymir* (15).

ଔ **GOAT:** Goat is another food sacred to Ásatrú. In the Lays of Hymiskvia and Gylfaginning, we are told how Thor kills the goats that pull his chariot to feast upon, and the next day they are alive again. Goat was also a main source for life-giving milk to our ancestors.

Appendix VII: Divine Association Runes and Colors

ᚱ Odin: Ansuz

ᚱ Freya: Fehu

ᚱ Frey: Ingwaz

ᚱ Tyr: Teiwaz

ᚱ Thor: Thurisaz

ᚱ Baldr: Dagaz

ᚱ Frigg: Berkano

ᚱ Nerthus: Jera

ᚱ Fenris: Uruz

ᚱ Hel: Ear

ᚱ Jörmundgand: Ior

If you want to use candles or decorate your altar for blóts, we suggest you try the following colors:

ᚱ Odin: deep blue

ᚱ Freya: green or red (depending on what aspect you are calling on. For Mayday or fertility it would be green. For her gifts of warcraft or seiðr it would be wise to use red.)

ᚱ Frey: green or golden

ᚱ Frigg: green or light blue

ᚱ Nerthus: green

ᚱ Thor: red

ᚱ Tyr: white

ᚱ Fenris: black or red

ᚱ Hel: black

ᚱ Baldr: yellow

ᚱ Jörmungand: aqua or sea-green

Appendix VIII: The futhorc Runes

Our kindred uses the Elder Futhark, but you should also be familiar with these Anglo-Frisian Futhorc runic system.

Anglo-Saxon Name	Norse Name	English Equivalent	
Feoh *(fay-oh)*	Fehu	F	ᚠ
Ur *(oor)*	Uruz	U	ᚢ
Thorn *(thorn)*	Thurisaz	Th	ᚦ
Aesc *(ash)*	Ansuz	A as in hat	ᚨ
Rad *(rahd)*	Raido	R	ᚱ
Ken *(ken)*	Kenaz	K or hard C	ᚲ
Gyfu *(gif-oo)*	Gebo	G	ᚷ
Wyn *(win)*	Wunjo	W or V	ᚹ
Haegl *(hay-gle)*	Hagalaz	H	ᚾ
Nyð *(neeth)*	Nauðiz	N	ᚾ
Is *(ice)*	Isa	I	ᛁ
Jer *(yair)*	Jera	J	ᛃ
Eoh *(ay-oh)*	Eihwaz	A as in hay	ᛇ
Peorth *(pay-orth)*	Perthro	P	ᛈ
Eolx *(ay-olks)*	Elhaz or Algiz	X, Z	ᛉ
Sigil *(see-gil)*	Sowelu	S	ᛋ
Tyr *(teer)*	Teiwaz	T	ᛏ
Beorc *(bay-orc)*	Berkana	B	ᛒ
Eh *(ehh)*	Ehwaz	E as in bed	ᛖ
Mann *(mahn)*	Mannaz	M	ᛗ
Laeg *(lag)*	Laguz	L	ᛚ
Ing *(ing)*	Ingwaz	Ng	ᛝ
Daeg *(dag)*	Dagaz	D	ᛞ
Oethel *(oy-thel)*	Othala	O as in box	ᛟ
Ear *(ee-ar or ay ar)*	None	E as in sea	ᛠ
Ac *(ahk)*	None	A as in father	ᚪ
Ior *(yor)*	None	Y as in yellow	ᛡ
Os *(ohss)*	None	O as in home	ᚩ

Yr (yeer or yerr)	None	Y as in funny, or Germanic ö	ᛦ
Cweorth *(cway-orth)*	None	Q	ᚳ
Chalc *(khalk)*	None	Ch, or gutteral H *(khh)*	ᛣ
Stan *(shtan)*	None	St or Sh	ᛥ
Gar	None	no sound associated	ᚸ

In thy home be joyous and generous to guests
discreet shalt thou be in thy bearing,
mindful and talkative, wouldst thou gain wisdom,
oft making me mention of good.
-The Hávámal

Appendix IX: The Younger Futhark

The Younger Futhark is a reduced form of the Elder Futhark. It is divided into two variants: Long Branch and Short Branch.

Long Branch:

F   U   Th A R   K   H   N   I   A   S   T B   M   L   R

Short Branch:

F   U   Th A R   K   H   N   I   A   S   T B   M   L   R

A better burden can no man bear
on the way than his mother wit;
'tis the refuge of the poor, and richer it seems
than wealth in a world untried.
-The Hávámal

Appendix X: The Anglo-Saxon Rune Poem

Feoh byþ frofur fira gehwylcum;
    sceal ðeah manna gehwylc miclun hyt dælan
    gif he wile for drihtne domes hleotan.

Ur byþ anmod ond oferhyrned,
    felafrecne deor, feohteþ mid hornum
    mære morstapa; þæt is modig wuht.

Ðorn byþ ðearle scearp; ðegna gehwylcum
    anfeng ys yfyl, ungemetum reþe
    manna gehwelcum, ðe him mid resteð.

Os byþ ordfruma ælere spræce,
    wisdomes wraþu ond witena frofur
    and eorla gehwam eadnys ond tohiht.

Rad byþ on recyde rinca gehwylcum
    sefte ond swiþhwæt, ðamðe sitteþ on ufan
    meare mægenheardum ofer milpaþas.

Cen byþ cwicera gehwam, cuþ on fyre
    blac ond beorhtlic, byrneþ oftust
    ðær hi æþelingas inne restaþ.

Gyfu gumena byþ gleng and herenys,
    wraþu and wyrþscype and wræcna gehwam
    ar and ætwist, ðe byþ oþra leas.

Wealth is a comfort to all men;
  yet must every man bestow it freely,
  if he wish to gain honour in the sight of the Lord.

The aurochs is proud and has great horns;
  it is a very savage beast and fights with its horns;
  a great ranger of the moors, it is a creature of mettle.

The thorn is exceedingly sharp,
  an evil thing for any knight to touch,
  uncommonly severe on all who sit among them.

The mouth is the source of all language,
  a pillar of wisdom and a comfort to wise men,
  a blessing and a joy to every knight.

Riding seems easy to every warrior while he is indoors
  and very courageous to him who traverses the high-roads
  on the back of a stout horse.

The torch is known to every living man by its pale, bright flame;
  it always burns where princes sit within.

Generosity brings credit and honour, which support one's dignity;
  it furnishes help and subsistence
  to all broken men who are devoid of aught else.

Wenne bruceþ, ðe can weana lyt
     sares and sorge and him sylfa hæfþ
     blæd and blysse and eac byrga geniht.

Hægl byþ hwitust corna;
     hwyrft hit of heofones lyfte,
     wealcaþ hit windes scura;
     weorþeþ hit to wætere syððan.

Nyd byþ nearu on breostan; weorþeþ hi þeah oft niþa bearnum
     to helpe and to hæle gehwæþre, gif hi his hlystaþ æror.

Is byþ ofereald, ungemetum slidor,
     glisnaþ glæshluttur gimmum gelicust,
     flor forste geworuht, fæger ansyne.

Ger byþ gumena hiht, ðonne God læteþ,
     halig heofones cyning, hrusan syllan
     beorhte bleda beornum ond ðearfum.

Eoh byþ utan unsmeþe treow,
     heard hrusan fæst, hyrde fyres,
     wyrtrumun underwreþyd, wyn on eþle.

Peorð byþ symble plega and hlehter
     wlancum [on middum], ðar wigan sittaþ
     on beorsele bliþe ætsomne.

Eolh-secg eard hæfþ oftust on fenne
     wexeð on wature, wundaþ grimme,
     blode breneð beorna gehwylcne
     ðe him ænigne onfeng gedeþ.

Bliss he enjoys who knows not suffering, sorrow nor anxiety,
  and has prosperity and happiness
  and a good enough house.

Hail is the whitest of grain;
  it is whirled from the vault of heaven
  and is tossed about by gusts of wind
  and then it melts into water.

Trouble is oppressive to the heart;
  yet often it proves a source of help and salvation
  to the children of men, to everyone who heeds it betimes.

Ice is very cold and immeasurably slippery;
  it glistens as clear as glass and most like to gems;
  it is a floor wrought by the frost, fair to look upon.

Summer is a joy to men, when God, the holy King of Heaven,
  suffers the earth to bring forth shining fruits
  for rich and poor alike.

The yew is a tree with rough bark,
  hard and fast in the earth, supported by its roots,
  a guardian of flame and a joy upon an estate.

Peorth is a source of recreation and amusement to the great,
  where warriors sit blithely together
  in the banqueting-hall.

The *Eolh*-sedge is mostly to be found in a marsh;
  it grows in the water and makes a ghastly wound,
  covering with blood
  every warrior who touches it.

Sigel semannum symble biþ on hihte,
      ðonne hi hine feriaþ ofer fisces beþ,
      oþ hi brimhengest bringeþ to lande.

Tir biþ tacna sum, healdeð trywa wel
      wiþ æþelingas; a biþ on færylde
      ofer nihta genipu, næfre swiceþ.

Beorc byþ bleda leas, bereþ efne swa ðeah
      tanas butan tudder, biþ on telgum wlitig,
      heah on helme hrysted fægere,
      geloden leafum, lyfte getenge.

Eh byþ for eorlum æþelinga wyn,
      hors hofum wlanc, ðær him hæleþ ymb[e]
      welege on wicgum wrixlaþ spræce
      and biþ unstyllum æfre frofur.

Man byþ on myrgþe his magan leof:
      sceal þeah anra gehwylc oðrum swican,
      forðum drihten wyle dome sine
      þæt earme flæsc eorþan betæcan.

Lagu byþ leodum langsum geþuht,
      gif hi sculun neþan on nacan tealtum
      and hi sæyþa swyþe bregaþ
      and se brimhengest bridles ne gym[eð].

Ing wæs ærest mid East-Denum
      gesewen secgun, oþ he siððan est
      ofer wæg gewat; wæn æfter ran;
      ðus Heardingas ðone hæle nemdun.

The sun is ever a joy in the hopes of seafarers
     when they journey away over the fishes' bath,
     until the courser of the deep bears them to land.

Tiw is a guiding star; well does it keep faith with princes;
     it is ever on its course
     over the mists of night and never fails.

The poplar bears no fruit; yet without seed it brings forth suckers,
     for it is generated from its leaves.
     Splendid are its branches and gloriously adorned
     its lofty crown which reaches to the skies.

The horse is a joy to princes in the presence of warriors.
     A steed in the pride of its hoofs,
     when rich men on horseback bandy words about it;
     and it is ever a source of comfort to the restless.

The joyous man is dear to his kinsmen;
     yet every man is doomed to fail his fellow,
     since the Lord by his decree will commit
     the vile carrion to the earth.

The ocean seems interminable to men,
     if they venture on the rolling bark
     and the waves of the sea terrify them
     and the courser of the deep heed not its bridle.

Ing was first seen by men among the East-Danes,
     till, followed by his chariot,
     he departed eastwards over the waves.
     So the Heardingas named the hero.

Eþel byþ oferleof æghwylcum men,
    gif he mot ðær rihtes and gerysena on
    brucan on bolde bleadum oftast.

Dæg byþ drihtnes sond, deore mannum,
    mære metodes leoht, myrgþ and tohiht
    eadgum and earmum, eallum brice.

Ac byþ on eorþan elda bearnum
    flæsces fodor, fereþ gelome
    ofer ganotes bæþ; garsecg fandaþ
    hwæþer ac hæbbe æþele treowe.

Æsc biþ oferheah, eldum dyre
    stiþ on staþule, stede rihte hylt,
    ðeah him feohtan on firas monige.

Yr byþ æþelinga and eorla gehwæs
    wyn and wyrþmynd, byþ on wicge fæger,
    fæstlic on færelde, fyrdgeatewa sum.

Iar byþ eafix and ðeah a bruceþ
    fodres on foldan, hafaþ fægerne eard
    wætre beworpen, ðær he wynnum leofaþ.

Ear byþ egle eorla gehwylcun,
    ðonn[e] fæstlice flæsc onginneþ,
    hraw colian, hrusan ceosan
    blac to gebeddan; bleda gedreosaþ,
    wynna gewitaþ, wera geswicaþ.

An estate is very dear to every man,
> if he can enjoy there in his house
> whatever is right and proper in constant prosperity.

Day, the glorious light of the Creator, is sent by the Lord;
> it is beloved of men,
> a source of hope and happiness to rich and poor,
> and of service to all.

The oak fattens the flesh of pigs for the children of men.
> Often it traverses the gannet's bath,
> and the ocean proves whether the oak keeps faith
> in honourable fashion.

The ash is exceedingly high and precious to men.
> With its sturdy trunk it offers a stubborn resistance,
> though attacked by many a man.

Yr is a source of joy and honour to every prince and knight;
> it looks well on a horse
> and is a reliable equipment for a journey.

Iar is a river fish and yet it always feeds on land;
> it has a fair abode encompassed by water,
> where it lives in happiness.

The grave is horrible to every knight,
> when the corpse quickly begins to cool
> and is laid in the bosom of the dark earth.
> Prosperity declines, happiness passes away
> and covenants are broken.

Appendix XI: Sigdrifa's Prayer Choral Music

This is the four-part choral version of Sigdrifa's Prayer, used by our Neo-Pagan church. This prayer (and its various translations) is the oldest surviving pagan Norse prayer, written by a woman named Sigdrifa in medieval times. The original melody was written by Galina Krasskova, and the choral arrangement was created by Raven Kaldera, with the original Old Norse words as the soprano descant and the tenors as an English harmony. The altos and the basses sing the melody together, so it can be used by either men's or women's groups who want to sing in unison—just pick bass or alto to figure out the melody, and transpose as you like. The soprano can be made a tenor part for an all-men's singing group, or the tenor harmony be made a soprano harmony (on top of the descant) for an all-women's group.

Old Norse words and pronunciation:
Heill Dagr! Heillir Dags synir! Heill Nótt og nift!
(Hayl dahg! Hayl dahgs sin-eer! Hayl Note ohg neeft!

Óreiðum augum littið okkur þinig
(Or-ay-thoom oy-goom lit-tith awh-koor thin-ig)

Og gefið sitjöndum sigur.
(Og gev-ith sit-yun-doom see-goor.)

Heilir Æsir! Heilar Ásynjur!
(Hayl-eer I-seer! Hayl-ar ow-seen-yoor!)

Heil sjá in fjölnýta fold!
(Hayl syah in fyul-nee-ta fold!)

Mal og manvit gefið okkur mærum tveim
(Mahl og man-veet gev-ith awh-koor my-room tvaym)

Og læknishendur meðan lifum.
(Og like-neesh-en-door may-than lee-voom.)

English translation:
Hail to the Day! Hail Day's sons!
Hail to Night and her daughters!
With loving eyes, look upon us here and bring us victory.

Hail to the sky Gods, hail to the sky Goddesses,

Hail to the mighty fecund Earth.

Eloquence and native wit bestow on us here,

And healing hands while we live.

Sigdrifa's Prayer

Arranged by Galina Krasskova and Raven Kaldera

Appendix XII: Guardians of Othala Contact Information

Most of the materials mentioned can be purchased from World Tree Publications, Post Office Box 961, Payson, Arizona 85547.

In conclusion, we wish to be treated as any other religious belief, with respect and dignity until otherwise demonstrated.

We are as one with nature, our Ancestors and our Gods.

Any other questions can be directed to:
Guardians of Othala
P.O. Box 216
Downers Grove, IL 60515
Email: guardiansofothala@gmail.com

Or with a self addressed envelope to:
Ásatrú Alliance
P.O. Box 961, Payson, Arizona 85547

Other Points of Contact:
Director of Chaplain's Service
Federal Bureau of Prisons
320 First Street, N.W.
Washington, D.C. 20534

Office of the Regional Chaplain
Federal Bureau of Prisons
For the North Central Region
Gateway Complex Tower II, 8th floor
4th and State Avenue
Kansas City, KS 66101-2492

References for the Sacred Lands section:
- *The Poetic Edda*, Lee M. Hollander
- *Edda*, Snorri Sturleson
- *Futhark*, Edred Thorsson

- ଜ *Runelore*, Edred Thorsson
- ଜ *Gods & Myths of Northern Europe*, H. R. Ellis Davidson
- ଜ *The Agricola & GerMánia*, Tacitus
- ଜ *The Lost Beliefs of Northern Europe*, H. R. Ellis Davidson
- ଜ *History of the Vikings*, Gwyn Jones
- ଜ *Rituals of Ásatrú,* Stephan McNallen, World Tree Publications

Not great things alone must one give to another,
Praise oft is earned for nought;
With half a loaf and a tilted jug
I have found me many a friend.
- The Hávámal